G000058207

MANNEQUIN

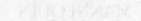

MANNEQUIN

Working Women in India's Glamour Industry

MANJIMA BHATTACHARJYA

ZUBAAN
128 B Shahpur Jat, 1st floor
NEW DELHI 110 049
Email: contact@zubaanbooks.com
Website: www.zubaanbooks.com

First published by Zubaan Publishers Pvt. Ltd 2018, in collaboration with the
New India Foundation
Copyright © Manjima Bhattacharjya 2018

All rights reserved

10 9 8 7 6 5 4 3 2 1

ISBN 978 93 85932 22 9

Zubaan is an independent feminist publishing house based in New Delhi with
a strong academic and general list. It was set up as an imprint of India's first
feminist publishing house, Kali for Women, and carries forward Kali's tradition
of publishing world quality books to high editorial and production standards.
Zubaan means tongue, voice, language, speech in Hindustani. Zubaan publishes
in the areas of the humanities, social sciences, as well as in fiction, general non-
fiction, and books for children and young adults under its Young Zubaan imprint.

Typeset by Jojy Philip, New Delhi 110 015
Printed at Replika Press Pvt. Ltd, India

To 'Vinita',
who opened doors for me in life and death

To JNU and Jagori,
my twin sites of resistance and learning

Contents

CHANGE

LAST WORDS

Foreword

A Feminist Spy in the House of Fashion

This book is based on my doctoral research from 2003 to 2007, a sociological study of women working in the Indian glamour industry as models. For almost seven years prior to this I had been an activist with a Delhi based feminist group, participating in several protests against the objectification of women's bodies. So why, you may ask, did I want to study something I was ideologically opposed to? This is a complicated question to answer.

One evening I chanced upon an episode of a television show called 'The Big Fight' (NDTV, 3rd April 2004). The topic for debate was: 'Are beauty pageants an exercise in futility?' On the panel was a former Miss World, a women's rights activist, the managing director of the corporate entity that organized the Miss India pageant, and an actor known for offbeat roles. The anchor was the (then) political editor of the channel. The debate went like this:

> *Former Miss World:* If women activists like you are so concerned with empowerment, why not use people like us to talk on those issues?
>
> *Women's Rights Activist:* You mean you don't know that there is female infanticide, dowry deaths, rape? Not one of the beauty queens has social commitment or has done what they said they would.

Managing Director: See, the pageants... It's about empowerment, marketability... It's a platform to show that Indian women are no less...

Audience (to Women's Rights Activist): You talk of the empowerment of women, but you forget that these women are showing that Indian women are as good as any in all parts of the world. (Some people in the audience break into applause.)

Actor in Offbeat Films: I'm shocked to hear you say that. These beauty queens hardly mean anything.... Women like Medha Patkar and Kiran Bedi represent women of India, not the Former Miss Worlds.

Former Miss World: I don't believe we are any less than anyone else – social workers, whatever. As individuals, we have an opinion. You women activists have fought so hard to get women like us where we are. To give voice to women. And now when we are have a voice you want to suppress us? If in the course of all this, we are of some use to cosmetic companies, what is the harm?

Anchor: But... women have to fake their lives in order to pursue this dream!

Former Miss World: I've been faking my life since I was fourteen. I said I was twenty to put food on the table. I worked because I had to.

I was intrigued. Even as the pageant organizers speaking for the beauty queens claimed it was about their empowerment, the beauty queen herself claimed she was a victim of circumstances. In a surprise move, she shifted the terms of the discussion to speak in a new language – of 'having to' work to put food on the table.

Beauty queens, 'working'?

Then, the tussle over who is the real Indian woman. For someone who is identified globally as Miss India, to be told that she does not represent 'real Indian women' must have come as a shock. Not to mention the disdain that she is less than them and her 'achievement' is questionable since there is little merit or real work involved.

By cleverly positing the beauty queen against a women's rights activist, the TV channel not only ensured a confrontation erupted, but also invoked the two as traditional 'enemies', as they have often been represented in Western history. It was at the Miss America pageant at Atlantic City in 1968 and 1969 where the infamous women's liberation protests took place, setting off a new wave of feminist activism in the USA.

Two things bothered me about this discussion. One was how, despite our lives being full of images of glamorous people and information on ways of becoming glamorous ourselves, factual information on the fashion world, and the experiences of women in it, were hard to come by. In the few fictionalized portrayals that began to come out around that time (a film on the industry, for example, by a Bollywood filmmaker that came out in 2008), the focus remained on the sensational and popular stereotypes aimed at grabbing eyeballs. The other was the pitting of women's rights (or women's rights activists) against women in the glamour industry. Was this division real or constructed?

Keeping the latter concern aside, it was these women's voices, so far absent, that I sought through my research. I wanted to know what brought them to this field of work, what 'work' they really did, how they negotiated public perceptions of who they were, how they felt about being seen as 'objects' – which was another perception promoted by certain strains of feminism. I wanted to write their stories from their points of view by taking a deep dive into their world, a method in social science research known as ethnography. But how would I do this? How would I gain access to their world, let alone be able to take a deep dive?

The Lakmé India Fashion Week (LIFW) in 2004 was my first point of contact with this world. I had wondered what would constitute 'the field' in this study (where primary data is gathered in a natural environment), and found that the fashion week came closest to a fixed moment and physical space where the disparate members of the glamour industry came together in some form.

LIFW lasted, by definition, 168 hours and was dismantled even as I was getting familiar with it. There was no time to 'settle', form relationships and observe at leisure from within, as traditional ethnography demands. I had to wait for one year before the 'field site' would reconstitute itself, although I knew it would not be the same field. The players would be new, relations would have to be rebuilt, a fresh beginning would have to be made.

At LIFW 2004 I was an outsider, my access limited to the public spaces. I had contacted the organizers of the event, Fashion Design Council of India (FDCI), earlier for passes to attend the morning seminars at the venue on 'The Business of Fashion', and they reluctantly agreed. Despite limited access there were opportunities to meet and interact with different people: the central place in the venue was a hotel lobby, a public space I could access. Over the days I was able to observe the industry play out, and approach models and designers for interviews later. I began building a database of contacts of models, agencies and other actors who agreed to be interviewed in the course of my fieldwork.

At LIFW 2005, I experienced the Fashion Week completely differently, by being an observer backstage in the green room through the week in which over 30 fashion shows took place.

I had decided to focus on women who were in the spotlight in the glamour industry, those in the profession of modelling. Over two years I undertook in-depth interviews with 30 women models ('respondents') at different stages of their career, including those who had participated and won in beauty contests. I also interviewed key informants of the industry, including editors of fashion and women's magazines, representatives from fashion retail giants, fashion show choreographers, model coordinators, and people in international modelling agencies.

Who were these women? Most of my respondents were based in Delhi, and some lived in Mumbai, the dual centres of the glamour industry. Many had moved to these cities from medium-sized towns like Agra, Varanasi, Bhopal or Delhi's satellite towns such as Faridabad and Ghaziabad, or from state capitals like Jaipur, Guwahati and Lucknow. One person claimed to be from 'a village' and two were Persons of Indian Origin (PIO) from outside India. Most came from modest, middle-class backgrounds. Only six out of 30 women interviewed were from well-off backgrounds.

The majority was Hindu, but there were also some women of Sikh, Christian and Islamic faith. Among the Hindus, almost a third were upper caste, while the rest were middle or from the dominant castes in their respective regions. Noticeably, none of the women I interviewed was from the Scheduled Caste or Scheduled Tribe categories or self-identified as Dalit. Most women's self-defined identities were drawn from other allegiances: their economic class, place of origin, occasionally their 'community' (such as 'Agarwal' or 'Kashimiri', mentioned only when talking about the constraints on girls from that community) their regional identity (as in the case of those from the North Eastern states in India) and whether they were from an armed forces background.

There is a perception in the industry that there is an over-representation of daughters of armed forces personnel in modelling, because people in the armed forces pay special attention to grooming and have a culture of pageantry in which daughters are encouraged to participate. However only three out of the 30 women interviewed came from an armed forces background.

The women I interviewed ranged from 17 to about 50 years of age. Four of them (Meera, Shirin, Niharika and Ritu) were 'first-generation' models. By 'generation' I refer to those who entered the industry around the same time or witnessed the industry at a particular moment in history, experiencing the same set of conditions.

The first generation comprised those who had worked as models in the late 1970s, through the 1980s and a bit of the early 1990s, at the beginning of the growth curve of the fashion industry. When I interviewed them, they were in their mid-thirties to early fifties, all English-speaking, convent or public school-educated, and married with children. In the first generation, there was a long period of general inactivity in the fashion world, before 1990 when India's economy opened up to foreign capital.

Six of the respondents (Honey, Mary, Josy, Noelle, Vinita and Naina) were 'second generation' models, between 25-30 years of age when I interviewed them. They had all started modelling in the mid-1990s after the onset of liberalization in India. All of them were still in the business when I met them, although they had started thinking about a Plan B, or other professions to segue into in a few years when their shelf life was likely to expire. This group was a real mix: graduates as well as those who had not finished their graduation; some married, some living-in with male partners and some single; English-speaking and non English-speaking, using a workable English learned over the years. No one in this group had children.

Respondents who made up the 'third generation' – seven of them (Nancy, Swati, Kavita, Leher, Kamal, Gurpreet and Ruhi) – were 22-28 years of age. They had joined the industry at the turn of the millennium, in 2000, when the industry had started changing rapidly. This group was also diverse, with a woman from a tribal community in the North East, a Haryanvi Jat and a Kashmiri Pandit. They were all graduates, some having obtained their degree through correspondence courses. All had done some sort of a vocational course too, such as 'cutting and tailoring' or 'media and communication'.

Thirteen respondents were from the 'fourth generation' having joined the industry from 2002 onwards, when the scenario changed with the entry of international modelling agencies (of the 13, Mayuri, Tina, Pragati, Mita, Heerina, Shivani, Natasha, Anupriya, Roopali and Palash feature in this book). Women in this group were 17-25 years old, some still studying in college. Five had dropped out of college, and one had dropped out of school.

The interviews were conducted in various places. Women invited me to their homes or met me in coffee shops or, in the odd case, five star hotels, and spent anything between an hour to sometimes four, sharing their life stories and reflections with me. If one interview was held in a model's smart suburban apartment with walls she had painted herself, the next would be in a dingy PG accommodation without windows, with space only for a mattress that became the woman's bed at night. One interview would be in a palatial apartment in Lutyens Delhi, another in a top-floor barsati in Lajpat Nagar, or at the bustling reception of a beauty salon that the respondent had started. Some multitasked while speaking – managing domestic help, juggling calls from clients or in-laws, handling a demanding child, at the same time finding a quiet space to settle down and talk to me over a cup of tea gone cold, the glamorous shell quietly taken off like a helmet.

For reasons of confidentiality, the names of the women used in all chapters are not their real names.

—w—

Once when I approached a producer of a televised model hunt for an interview, she said, 'If you're going to ask judgmental type of stuff then I'd rather not,' refusing to meet me until she was convinced I wasn't about to turn up at the Star TV building in Mumbai with a horde of placarding activists. As it turns out, I was indeed concerned about judging those I interviewed, because historically feminism and fashion have been pitted against one another. I was aware that the existing system defined unrealistic standards of 'beauty' and promoted unhealthy body images for women, focused on profit over anything else, and used certain tropes of desirability and sexiness to sell products. It appeared to reduce women from thinking beings to bodies for display. And I struggled to understand why women would participate in something that seemed to not value them as human beings. This was my central ideological turmoil.

I found as I went along that ethnography as a method enabled me to keep ideology outside the door when I entered into conversation with the women, because it allowed for them to speak their minds reflectively and invite me into their worlds, thus becoming more than just 'models'. Moreover I found that everyone was always judging everyone – based on how they looked, how they spoke, what they wore. It's not as if I was being judged any less. If I took offence at an editor of a women's magazine dismissing feminist protesters as 'ugly mothers of ugly daughters' in an interview, I kept my peace. Caricaturing feminists as 'ugly' was one of the oldest tricks in the book, one that feminists from the time of the suffragettes fighting for women's right to vote, had been subject to. Stereotypes about feminists – man hating, without a sense of humour, whatever – came with the territory.

But if feminists were targeted with stereotypes, so was fashion, trailed by ghosts of vanity, drugs, excess. The way through this dumpyard of prejudice was dialogue. Spending more and more time in the greenrooms and talking to women in the fashion world, these imaginary lines of battle drawn between us began to fade and I was able to see them, hear them, understand them as above all: young women chasing their dreams.

Young, *working* women chasing their dreams.

MEMORY

It is not memory, not the recollection of the past that is sacred, but the values that can be drawn from it.

– Tzvetan Todorov, 'Duties and Delights' 2009[1]

CHAPTER ONE

A Short and Personal History of Glamour in India

When did glamour come to India? Some would say it's always been there: Madhubala's smile, a maharaja's Rolls Royce collection, a maharani's pearls. Fashion too: Sadhna's haircut, the Nehru jacket. Certainly there was an inherent glamour in our over a hundred-year-old celluloid history and the lifestyles of former royals. But the contemporary version of glamour exceeds the coterie of royalty and film stars, permeating different spheres around us: images, billboards, clothes, make-up, magazines, gadgets, homes, bags, shoes.

'As a word, glamour carries talismanic qualities,' wrote historian Stephen Gundle in his book on the history of glamour,[2] 'a magical power capable of making ordinary people, dwellings and places seem like magnificent versions of themselves.' Gundle identifies a series of historic images, icons and moments that, when accumulated, contributed to the popularly understood idea of glamour in the West: Jackie Onassis, Marilyn Monroe, Princess Diana; designer Gianni Versace making a relatively unknown model, Elizabeth Hurley, a sensation overnight by putting her in a dress made of safety pins; finally defining glamour as 'a language of allure and seduction in capitalist society.'

But how and why did glamour emerge? What were the economic, political and social conditions that allowed it to flourish? How did it snowball into an economy generating magazines, pageants, television programming, a retail revolution, even a deeper shift in values from parsimony and unselfconsciousness to conspicuous consumption and giving unquestionable importance to looking good?

There are several key turning points that contributed to the mainstreaming of glamour in the West. First, the Belle Epoque (the 'beautiful age') in late 1800s Europe caused a seismic shift when music, theatre and the high arts became desirable forms of leisure for the new bourgeoisie, and drove a culture of 'going out' and couture. Second, around the same time the portraiture of high society women in the latest fashions flourished in Europe, creating the foundations of fashion photography.

Third, you might say: Paris.

Paris, with its cafés, concerts, new forms of leisure, rose as the incomparable glittering cultural capital of the world. Every city thereafter wanted to be Paris.

Fourth, the emergence of the commercial shopping and cultural district, the West End in London, in the early 1930s accelerated this shift with the spread of these ideas to the working class, away from bourgeouis monopolies. In the 1940s and 50s, glamour came galloping with the post-World War economic restructuring that emphasized shopping as leisure (and central to new economies) with scores of freshly minted departmental stores in New York and London. Such evolving ideas of modernity, of what urban metropolitan cities should symbolize, and ideas of leisure and pleasure lay at the heart of a new language of glamour.

Finally, and very importantly, technological advancements at every turn – the electrification of theatres, the creation of neon lights, television and then Technicolour – raised the stakes to showcase glamour and seductively mount it over every city and town, and later stream it into homes.

—∞—

1981 was an important year for me. I had my first experience of witnessing hysteria over a young boy called Kumar Gaurav whose hit film *Love Story* was the rage that summer; my brother was born;

and very importantly, a TV entered my grandparents' middle class home in the quiet, leafy Chittaranjan Park locality in New Delhi. It was the first TV I ever saw, a precious black and white ECTV with ribbed sliding shutters over its screen, complete with a little key. It arrived with ceremony, albeit discreetly. Television was a milestone in heralding glamour's tentative first steps into our living rooms.

In the 1970s and 1980s, when we wanted a dose of glamour, we bought a *Filmfare* or a *Stardust* at a railway station, or tuned in for the weekly medley of film songs in 'Chitrahaar' if we had a TV. With television's entry into middle class homes in the 1980s, glamour was closely linked with television advertising played on state owned channels.

Advertising was a small industry operating largely out of Bombay. Commercials were shot there, usually with local models, by a limited number of filmmakers, photographers and Bombay-based advertising agencies.

Models for these ads were recruited by 'spotting' young women in colleges and public places in Bombay where the agencies, filmmakers and photographers were based, or at the Miss India pageants. These pageants, held by two women's magazines, *Femina* and *Eve's Weekly* (based out of Bombay), were sparsely contested. Often, contestants had to be pursued, cajoled and personally invited to participate by the editors of the magazines.

Fashion shows in India have a scattered and barely-documented history. The earliest we hear of are Sylla and Nergish Spencer, or the 'Spencer Sisters' as they were known, who put together dazzling shows for select audiences in the 1950s. Then came the era of 'Jeannie and her Girls'. Jeannie Naoroji was known to be the grande dame of fashion shows who, with her troupe of models in the 1960s, presented choreographed fashion shows of different kinds: 'ship shows' held in luxury liners docking in Bombay's port, exhibiting Western designs but with Indian textiles or embroidery; 'travelling shows' or tours across the country organized by textile mills to advertise and sell a newly launched textile; 'fundraising shows' with dancing and spectacle for a cause; and niche shows for a select clientele, such as the opening of shopping arcades at five-star hotels such as the Oberoi or Taj.

Jeannie's Girls were expected to be Jills-of-all-trades – dancers, performers, graceful gliders (usually barefoot, the era of high heels was still to come) and costume wearers, all recruited by Jeannie and her hawk-eyed assistants. They were college girls from elite South Bombay colleges, secretaries in advertising agencies, young women spotted by the assistants in markets or movie halls, telephone operators or friends' daughters. This motley crew of amateurs were not always conventionally beautiful, but almost always 'Westernized', and always graceful.

Jeannie's monopoly was broken in the early 1980s by newer choreographers, including some from Delhi, who brought other skills to the presentation of a show: lights, stagecraft and the pizzazz of theatrical production. Vidyun Singh was one of them. She and her business partner Asha Kochhar went on to become pioneers of the choreographed fashion shows as we know them today. In her Delhi office, neatly filed with boxes of paperwork from shows done over the past decade, she reminisced about her big break: 'There used to be Trade Fair shows at that time in Pragati Maidan, where every November for a month there would be an evening slot for a fashion show. It was the *hugest* draw. And that time, the shows would be from Bombay, because there was no person in Delhi who was considered to be at par. Jeannie Naoroji and Vimla Patil from *Femina*, they would be getting contracts and doing the shows. And I have to repeat: they were the hugest draws at the Trade Fair. So when my partner and I did a presentation before the committee and got our first show at the Trade Fair, it was a big deal.'

Vidyun and Asha had a theatre and stagecraft background, and pitched for the Trade Fair contract after some experience of producing and choreographing such shows at the college level. 'We were just lucky,' she says of the success that came later, and of the vocation that within a decade became their playground. 'In hindsight, nobody thought it would be as big as it has become today. We were in the right place at the right time.' Vidyun and Asha's business flourished through the 1980s, supported largely through state-sponsored shows that promoted handicrafts – sometimes for tourism, sometimes for trade in textiles. 'The government support was a lot more at that time. It could be the textile corporation, handloom promotion board, or even a collaboration with a state emporium highlighting a particular fabric. We had textile-driven and not designer-driven fashion shows,' says Vidyun.

This wasn't surprising, considering that a central element of the contemporary fashion show was entirely missing in this era: the fashion designer. This problem was soon solved when the state set up the National Institute of Fashion Technology (NIFT) under the Ministry of Textiles in 1986 in Delhi, with a vision of 'establishing Indian textiles and Indian fashion on the world stage'. From this was to come India's first batch of official fashion designers.

By the end of the 1980s all the elements were coming together to create a fertile ground for the birth of a new era of fashion and glamour. The fashion show had evolved from a song-and-dance affair to a presentation of textiles and garments. A new breed of professionals had risen who were 'choreographers' of these shows. Fashion design had been introduced into the system, even institutionalized, and the first batches of fashion designers were getting ready to wiggle their toes in Indian waters. Television had become a central part of people's lives, reaching remote corners of the country. Advertising, as a result, was doing extremely well; and increasingly, a lexicon of images – a bikini-clad Karen Lunel (the 'Liril Girl') under a waterfall, the Garden Vareli ladies swirling in swathes of chiffon, the Charminar man astride his bike with pillion-riding girlfriend – was entering the mainstream to help us define this new form of glamour. The stage was set.

—⁓—

As the 1990s rolled in, violence entered our lives. Within a few months, it became clear that this was going to be a difficult time for India. Governments rose and fell. Prime ministers were shuffled – V.P. Singh, Chandra Shekhar, finally settling on the government of P.V. Narasimha Rao. Significant blows were struck, one after the other, within a few years. Young students burned themselves in public squares protesting reservation for marginalized castes as suggested by the Mandal Commission, causing schools and colleges to shut down for months. The former Prime Minister, Rajiv Gandhi, was assassinated by a suicide bomber in Tamil Nadu. The Babri Masjid was demolished by a prominent right wing political party, triggering communal riots in many parts of the country.

As if our cup of woes was not full enough, the country was reeling under a financial crisis. In July 1991, the Congress government led by Prime Minister P.V. Narasimha Rao announced that, regretfully, India was on the brink of bankruptcy, primarily because of a balance-of-payments crisis. To manage the situation, he announced a slew of economic reforms (devaluing the rupee, structural adjustments and liberal economic policies) in exchange for a bailout from the International Monetary Fund. He made the analogy that like a blocked artery needed a bypass surgery, this too would be a 'bypass' to deal with the crisis at hand. Previous Congress governments had shown a 'tendency to globalize' yet had not completely thrown open Indian doors to foreign capital. But this heralded a new phase in Indian economic history. It marked a paradigmatic shift in Indian development policy and national vision, away from the socialist planned development to one in which there was a greater role for the free market.

Did the ugly realities around us make Indians yearn for some beauty? Did we want some distraction from the destruction and chaos? Was it that things were falling apart and we needed some glue to keep the country intact? Did we need a shot in the arm of some uplifting substance? The high of nationalism and retail-therapy? This shot in the arm came soon after, as Indians watched on cable TV, serial wins at the Miss World and Miss Universe pageants that buoyed national sentiments.

A series of overlapping coincidences after 1990, the year India dismantled its barriers to foreign capital, or got 'globalized', helped bring glamour further into our lives. As satellite media arrived, television became all-pervasive. Import-export restrictions were lifted, and items that had earlier been luxury goods with high levels of taxation, began to enter the market at affordable prices. This was accompanied by a boom in advertising, driven by multinational products entering the Indian market, the explosion of TV channels due to satellite media and the entry of many new magazines. Music channels with smart, international-looking VJs brought pop culture and Western fashion into the world of young Indians. In addition, the advertising industry had developed significantly by now, and began to look outside Bombay for new faces.

As the NIFT experiment proved successful, new fashion designers became rich and famous. Private fashion design schools came up across the country, giving an impetus to design as a profession. This, in turn, led to renewed interest in the 'fashion show' as a forum for the showcasing of clothes designed by the growing breed of designers. Ramp modelling came into prominence in 1989, when international fashion houses from Europe, Pierre Cardin and Yves Saint-Laurent, came to India. With the media build-up around this, and the selection of some Indian models to go to Paris, ramp models came into the spotlight.

Meanwhile, India saw spectacular international success at beauty pageants in 1994 when two young women, the 19-year old Sushmita Sen and the 21-year old Aishwarya Rai, won the titles of Miss Universe and Miss World respectively. Social commentator Madhu Kishwar wrote caustically that Indians were celebrating like Americans did when Neil Armstrong landed on the moon.[3]

Even though the 1994 wins were perceived as being the turning point, it was the preceding years that were actually the game-changers. The 1990s saw a change in the demographics of participants in pageants. No longer just elite South Bombay college girls, they were now a wider, more diverse group. Girls from non English-speaking middle classes took to modelling: one of them, Madhu Sapre, came from a traditional Maharashtrian family. She won the Miss India title, later garnering third position in the Miss Universe contest in 1992. Following this taste of international success, the organizers of the Miss India pageant recognized the potential of this enterprise and raised the prize money from 7,000 to 100,000 rupees the very next year. 1993 was also the first year the pageant was telecast live, thereby transforming it from a local Bombay event to a national phenomenon beamed into every home with a television.

With Sapre's win and the consequent world titles feted globally, these women became the role models for many girls from modest socio-economic backgrounds. It was clear that an elite background was no longer necessary to be successful – the requisites could be acquired with dedication and exposure. As the profile of the participants changed, so did the preparation for international pageants by the organizers. Beauty pageants now became a serious business venture with high stakes and multiple sponsors.

—∞—

'The time was ripe,' says Sathya Saran, then editor of the women's magazine that organized the Miss India pageant. 'Indian women were CRAVING glamour'. Sathya was instrumental in transforming *Femina*, a magazine that had been a housewife's trusted monthly into a vehicle for glamour. She had two silver bullets. With one, she was going to make Miss Indias the next big thing. With the other, she would shoot holes into the drudgery and domesticity of the middle class Indian woman and do something no-one had done before: make her feel good. 'We (the magazine) weren't very glamorous ourselves when we realized that the Indian woman was craving glamour. We started helping her decide whether Indian products are making it up to the grade with foreign products, letting her pick the right things off the shelf, giving her know-how. Not being *critical* of her but being informative, being like a consultant.'

The magazine upped their beauty pages from two to 15. The 'upping' of fashion and beauty pages coincided with the entry of several new cosmetics and lifestyle products in the market in the country, and within months the two were intimately entwined. It was a marriage made in heaven. 'Big names were coming in because now the market was ready. The Indian woman was ready.'

Which 'Indian woman' was she catering to? Sathya says, 'The urban Indian woman. The aspirational Indian woman who wants to look better, feel better, be a better partner, worker, colleague, whatever. We are talking to HER. And beauty is part of her arsenal for being better.'

But the promotion of Western products doesn't mean she compromises on Indian values, Sathya stresses. 'I'm telling my readers: don't "progress" at the cost of anything else. You want to be Western, be Western. But it doesn't mean that when you see an elder person you don't touch their feet. It means that yes, you are old enough to take a flight and go to another city, and say, I am doing business tonight, tomorrow morning I'll come back. You are bold enough to ask your husband to take care of your child while you go out tonight. You are bold enough to tell your employer, buddy, I need this cash, if you can't give it to me I am finding another job. That is being Western, it's not saying, I don't care, and putting your parents in an old persons' home. It's not saying, I don't care, I'm using plastic because everyone in the West is using plastic.'

With the introduction of this cocktail of binaries into the magazine – the material West and spiritual East – circulation numbers began to rise in thousands. Or 'THOUSANDS' as she says. 'Circulation was 63,000 when I took over in 1992. In one year it doubled.'

If these ambitions for the urban, aspirational Indian women were still modest, her drive to make Miss Indias 'World Ambassadors' was less so. Conspiracy theorists may think the boom in Indian beauty queens was driven by a world awakening to the potential of India as a market for their beauty products, but not Sathya. 'No no that's not true, India did not happen because it was opening up as a market,' she says, 'India happened because we made it happen from here.' She waves a delicate wrist around her, indicating the office and the building that houses the media giant.

'Here inside the walls of this building.'

—m—

The old issues of *ELLE* India are stuck together in random bunches and bound in hard cover volumes in deep greens and maroons. The office boy helps me bring up the volumes from 1996-2000 to a private room away from the magazine office that is buzzing in the run-up to production week. Four years in the life of an international fashion magazine in India, imperceptible in the giant folds of time. But when stretched out like canvas on a frame these four years unfold to show some patterns.

As I read issues from 1996 up until the new millenium, I see a changing vocabulary: from images that focus on faces to those that focus on bodies. From more text to more images. From articles on the local Fashion Street to articles on Gucci. A changing mix of Indian and Western content, and experiments with what the fusion of the two could mean.

ELLE first came out in India as a bimonthly magazine in December 1996. The first issue cost 50 rupees and had 194 pages of which about 35 were ads: Dior perfumes, Piaget watches, Lakme products, Big Jo's and Shopper's Stop (the only departmental stores at the time stocking lifestyle products), ads for designers Rohit Bal and Shahab Durazi, and readers' contests, 'Win a diamond bracelet or a free trip to Paris'.

Early issues of *ELLE* have several conversations with models on what modelling is like. A report of the *ELLE* fashion show 1997 brings forth an interesting exchange between the report's author, Indian model Gauri Parulelkar, and Charlotte, the French choreographer of the show over the first item given to Gauri to wear, a sheer garment by designer Paco Rabanne.

Charlotte, with limited English: 'No bra. Okay?'

Gauri, regretful but firm: 'No, it is not okay… I am sorry. With a bra or change the outfit.'

Caroline, head-shake: 'It is your choice. C'est India.'

Gauri writes: 'My eyes lock hers in sympathy, in awareness: my India, land of dichotomy where the *Kamasutra* and the Purdah profess opposing truths. And I, slave to convention and professionalism, come at a price.'

Occasionally you read of what it's like to work in the fashion world. MTV VJ at the time and model Meghana Reddy says of her work, 'They shoot summer clothes in winter and vice-versa.'

At the end of 1997, ads from Cartier and Versace start coming up more regularly with luxury advertising from Oberoi. Indian catwalk images start getting more visible although they still stand apart rather awkwardly from the international catwalk pages.

Through 1998 the number of ads snowballs as does the presence of Indian celebrities – people from the ad world, fashion designers. The glamour quotient is on the rise but it's still possible to catch a 'serious' thread in the narratives. New advertisers include multi designer stores like Ogaan and Vama where new Indian designers are retailing. The content inside, and the cover girls on the outside, are still a charming mix of East and West. The online world starts making its presence felt as early as July 1998, when a website is advertised.

For the first time in December 1998, a Caucasian woman is on the cover. The issue is celebrating two years of publishing in India with a focus on international fashion and global fashion icons. With the January 1999 issue, the mission seems to have become clearer: to take Indian readers on a pilgrimage past Western fashion houses and icons – taking us into their homes, showing us images of their personal contexts, telling us their history, initiating us into a new market. Hollywood makes its presence felt as pictures of Nicole Kidman and Gwyneth Paltrow endorsing luxury brands start to bookend the issues.

The issues through 1999 are much more about the body, as the covers show. Six of the 12 covers are of the body: in a bikini, a wet monsoon look, a pregnant model, a bare back-shot.

A recurring strain is the expanding idea of what is glamorous, stylish, fashionable, whether it is tennis, F1 racing, doing the salsa or the *ELLE* style awards. India is still about textiles while foreign designers are houses of fashion.

Bollywood so far has been fairly conspicuous by its absence but the March 1999 issue has actor Karisma Kapoor on the cover in a sky blue satin shirt. Unthinkably, there is no mention of the brand of her clothes or make up, the photo focusing on her face. The next month returns to having models on the cover until a large shift later that year. The new millennium is welcomed with Aishwarya Rai, former Miss World and now Bollywood glamour girl (with a major hit film that year), on the cover. This is not her first time. Much has changed however since she was a cover girl in 1997 as the face of the local cosmetics brand Lakmé. In 2000 she would be the face of international brands L'Oréal and Longines, and the face of a new India. As *ELLE* India calls her in the special issue of January 2000: 'Globelle'.

—〜〜—

By 2000 fashion shows were being presented differently. A longer ramp replicating the Western runway replaced the traditional stage at fashion shows. In the past, models had done their own make-up or brought their own accessories for shows. But now, a battery of specialists supported each event: make-up artistes, hair stylists, colourists, fashion and accessory stylists formed the line-up backstage to attend to each model according to the creative brief given by the designer and choreographer.

At the same time, these shows continued to be a form of 'entertainment' at college festivals or cultural programmes. No occasion was too small to have a fashion show. But the year 2000 was significant for another reason: the advent of the India Fashion Week.

Fashion weeks emerged at the tail of the Second World War, when with Paris under siege, American fashion magazines fed on the opium of French couture faced a miserable slump in 'inspiration'. An enterprising journalist and fashion publicist took advantage of this and brought together American designers, to showcase their work for what she called 'Press Week', erecting massive white tents in which they could run their designs past American fashion followers. Over the years this became the historical New York Fashion Week, which continues to be held in luminous white tents.

New York, Paris, Milan, Singapore, Dubai, Sao Paolo, Moscow, Rio de Janeiro – today round the year, there is a calendar of fashion weeks set out for the international fashion industry, the 'season' beginning with New York Fashion Week and ending with Paris Fashion Week. These week-long events pack in scores of fashion shows by both new and well known designers from that country or city showcasing their designs. It is where retail giants select commercially viable trends and place bulk orders for their stores for the forthcoming season, setting international fashion trends.

The first such fashion week in India was called Lakmé India Fashion Week (LIFW) named after the main sponsor of the event, Indian cosmetics giant Lakmé. It was held in New Delhi, after the newly formed Fashion Design Council of India (FDCI, formed in 1998, with the aim of 'fostering growth of the Indian Fashion Industry with support from the Ministry of Textiles and other related Government bodies') contracted International Management Group (IMG) – the 'world's largest sport, lifestyle and entertainment marketing company' and also the organizers of New York Fashion Week – to conceive, organize and market India's first fashion week. In the next few years, LIFW came to be established as the fashion industry's most important calendar event for various stakeholders – the designers, sponsors, retailers, media and to some extent, models – which not only created a platform and provided the infrastructure to showcase and introduce Indian design talent, but also promoted the business potential of the fashion industry.

—ᴍ—

The Gladrags contest was started in the early 1990s by Maureen Wadia, wife of industrialist Nusli Wadia, owner of Bombay Dyeing, one of India's largest and oldest textile companies. While the company was already sponsoring something at the Miss India pageant, Maureen saw the business potential of having a Miss India of sorts of her own to promote their textile products. This wasn't that new a connection either, with textile mills having a history of hosting some of the first fashion shows. She began the Gladrags magazine, calling itself a fashion magazine but more modelled on the lines of men's magazines with images of models in swimsuits being one of its draws. One of the main events that the magazine undertook was the annual Gladrags Manhunt and Megamodel contest – an instant success, later spreading the web of beauty pageantry over a larger area to include the Mrs India, Little Miss and Master contests.

The company would in this way have an unending source of models for their various brands (the magazine, the bath and bed linen products), and in turn the winners would get visibility and a leg up into the modelling or film industries. The Gladrags success rested largely on the swimsuit round rather than a question-answer round, the winner ending up on the cover of the magazine. And while the Miss Indias turned their nose up at the contest, it was a more real alternative for many contenders. With little emphasis on being well spoken, it was about having a good leg of thigh. As some of its winners went on to join the film industry, it positioned itself as a suitable conduit to possible stardom.

Meanwhile, several international model hunts were also settling into the Indian contest landscape to scout for profitable faces and bodies from the region that they could display back in their markets as exotic fare. In 1994, *Femina* had tied up with Elite modelling agency to send models for the Elite Model Look annual contest, in which model Sheetal Mallar was among the top 15 given international contracts by Elite. Two years later, another model, Ujjwala Raut also went on to win an international contract, walking the ramp for international fashion brands in Milan. However, the Elite Model Look contest was discontinued in India until 2004, when it was brought back by the newly set up Elite India modelling agency.

Metropolitan, the French agency famous for 'finding' Claudia Schiffer and Eva Herzegovina, had launched an India model hunt in 2003 because Indian skin and looks were suddenly being preferred in the international market. Ford, another international agency with more supermodel 'finds' in their CV, entered the fray in 2004 with a contest of their own, called 'Supermodel of the World'.[4] 'India is a brand,' their Indian collaborator said, 'We believe that the next international supermodel will be from India.' Ford was clear it was an 'international beauty' they were looking for, even if it was in India, and so they insisted on keeping to their international criterion – a height at least of 175 cm (a condition that many years ago had prevented their own 'finds' Aishwarya Rai[5] and Bipasha Basu in a one-off scouting effort in India from participating in their international contest). However, 'in keeping with local sentiments' they had made a small change in their minimum age – while 14 was the minimum age for contestants in other countries, in India this was raised to 16.

These contests distinguished themselves by offering exceptionally lucrative prize monies. But they also dangled a carrot that now mattered much more than a diamond tiara or sash that said 'Miss Universe' or 'Miss World': an international modelling contract.

—m—

In 2004, ten years after the Miss Universe and Miss World double whammy, it was no longer the Miss India contest that was the talk of the town. It was the promos of a new TV show by a music channel, Channel V, that showed the metamorphosis of a plain bug into a sparkling butterfly with crystal encrusted, pink gossamer wings. The show was called Get Gorgeous and was one of the first model hunts in the country in the form of a reality TV show. 'No Casting Couch', the ads promised.

'What's a music channel doing hunting for models?' asked one participant's model sister. 'I thought it was a VJ hunt, not a model hunt,' said a confused participant in the first season. The first batch of Get Gorgeous girls may have been confused by this seeming incongruity, but later batches and a growing demographic of a young audience took to it like fish to water, quickly recognizing that it was not the modelling which the TV channel was keen on but the explosive possibilities of a reality show with a bevy of nervous beauties in high pressure situations.

In the inaugural season in 2004 the channel received some five to six thousand entries. Sixteen finalists were chosen from among these and taken to Goa for a televised competition. Four winners took home a contract with an international modelling agency and a chance to walk the ramp at Milan Fashion Week.

Namya, one of the producers of the first season of Get Gorgeous, explained the format of the show in her crisp style, 'It's a platform, a talent hunt cum reality show, with no precedent really, we didn't want to model it after anything else that was around. In the show the finalists were taught the business of modelling – ramp walk, basic make-up, style according to body type, fitness.

The girls had a five-day crash course with experts in the field, followed by a series of surprise competitions, a mock fashion show, and photo shoots, all televised.'

The screening process itself was novel. Besides formally applying, girls could also 'audition' by turning up for specially organized parties at night-clubs in seven cities where a scouting team would be shortlisting girls who had come for the party and 'auditioning' them on the spot. 'There were over 5000 applicants for sure,' Namya exclaims, 'There were stacks of letters everywhere! From all parts of the country, from all communities. Through the parties, through applications by post, through the net.' Finalists of the age group 16 to 25 years were selected 'on the basis of height, vital stats, face, body structure, shoulders, and general promise' by virtue of their personality.

The series found instant success, and continued to grow season to season, experimenting with the format, introducing celebrity visits, calling in a blogger to live amongst the girls and get behind-the-scenes videos, promising to be 'bigger, better, bolder' – moving with the times. The popularity of the show was considerable; Season 5 in 2008 was said to have had 10 million viewers.

—m—

Circa 2005, and it was no longer sufficient to call the making and consuming of glamour an 'industry'. A Big Bang had taken place and made fashion a full blown economy, a universe unto itself. Core businesses in this economy included the Miss India pageant, the fashion weeks and the advertising industry. Attached to each of these planets was a retinue of moons: sponsors, hotels, event management companies, film production houses, professional speech and diction experts, gym trainers, choreographers, hair treatment experts, skin experts, dental procedure experts, cosmetic surgery consultants, photographers and so on. Models were the extra-terrestrials that floated between these businesses, often with the help of model coordinators or agencies that managed them. Along with this expansion of the field, there existed a differentiation in the kind of models suitable for different kinds of assignments –

television, print or ramp – and for different markets. The director of an international modelling agency said, 'My Bombay models are totally different from the Delhi models. Delhi is all about fashion shows, and Bombay is all TV commercials and serials. In Bombay there is no height criteria, you don't have to be absolutely skinny, you don't need to walk the ramp, you don't need to have that ramp attitude… you have to look like the conventional pretty girl-next-door with a dazzling smile. For the international market, the look is very different. What the West wants is a very anonymous kind of look – someone who would keep people guessing where she's from. That's a global look. And it's a very bland kind of look. But that doesn't work for the local market.'

There was also the differentiation of body parts. In the advertising industry, all sorts of body part shots were being outsourced to second-tier models (called 'body models'), from the hair, hands, feet, to the back, chest and even underarms,[6] as it reduced costs and solved the problem of bigger actors or models waiting around for a 'simple hand shot'. Images that appeared as a whole (to the viewer say, a beauty queen advertising jewellery) were actually an assemblage of body parts of different persons; the hand on which the ring dazzled was not necessarily hers.

The glamour economy interacted with a global and local market. International retail stores like Selfridges (UK) and Saks Fifth Avenue (USA) often held India-themed shopping festivals. Other countries, especially with sizeable Indian populations, such as in the Middle East, also have a high demand for Indian designer wear. Various international design and retail houses (including Armani, Versace and Zandra Rhodes) outsourced their embroidery, beading and other piecework to Indian designers and craftspeople. This back-end integration has been in process for many years now. Hollywood also outsourced some of its costume design work to Indian shores.

The fashion industry was linked to the local 'underground' market that was famous for copies of designer wear, particularly traditional wedding garments. Copies of bridal outfits by well-known designers could be bought in markets such as Delhi's Chandni Chowk or Karol Bagh for one-fifth of the original's cost, and, though a contested issue in design circles, for many designers, the real test of their success was a copy of their design in a low-end store. Also vital was the industry's link with the media and satellite television, which, in fact, performed one of the most important functions of the glamour economy: embedding it in the public consciousness and ensuring consumption.

—◦◦◦—

Vogue India launched in 2007 with 12 Bollywood stars on their cover, a startling expression of the blitzkrieg that Bollywood had waged on the industry. As if there were no Indian models worthy of being on the cover of *Vogue* India.

—◦◦◦—

In 2009, Fashion Week celebrated its tenth year. The first Men's Fashion Week was launched as part of it. India Fashion Weeks moved determinedly towards mainstreaming into the international market as designers started showcasing collections in the international format (that is, one season in advance). But not without retaining a certain 'Indianness' about them through increased intertwining with Bollywood, which was going through its own fashion evolution, moving from garish costumery to stylized designer togs. Often a 'showstopper' from Bollywood ended a show. Film stars were anointed to sit on the front row wearing clothes designed by the designer whose show they were at (sometimes from the collection they were just showing – demonstrating that they had special access). Being invited to be a 'finale designer' (the last show of Fashion Week) was a badge of privilege often given to the more prominent enfant terrible or shining light of the fashion world.

By 2012 it seemed there was trouble in paradise. A columnist for a national daily (Vinod Nair writing 'Tailor Talk') noted how the boom was 'ruining the sanctity of fashion weeks'. Designers lamented that the avalanche of fashion weeks was burning them out. 'When will we work if we're just going for fashion weeks?' one of them asked. Nair wrote of how one designer (Rahul Mishra) was invited to participate in seven fashion weeks over one year: Wills India Lifestyle Fashion Week, Van Heusen Men's Fashion Week in Delhi, Lakmé Fashion Week in Mumbai, Bangalore Fashion Week, India Couture Week and the Goa Resort Week. He chose to participate in two: Wills India Lifestyle Fashion Week for business, and Lakmé Fashion Week for the publicity.

Smaller retailers did not however find the multiple fashion weeks a problem. Localized fashion weeks in smaller cities had sprung fresh local talent, and buyers in the region no longer felt it was necessary to go to Delhi or Bombay to stock designer stores.

Overall the fashion industry was recording unprecedented growth: touching a turnover of 7.5 billion rupees in 2011[7] and maintaining a high growth rate since, of between 10 to 12 per cent annually. The industry was expected to bring in 3940 billion rupees by 2020 in India,[8] although the global fashion industry appeared to have hit a rough patch.[9] More recently, the expansion from one sector to another has been remarkable. Fashion weeks have expanded beyond clothes or certain types of clothes: from couture to bridal wear to jewellery and now, the flavour of the season, textiles and new-age designer handlooms. In a way, full circle to its origins in India.

—⁂—

We are living in a 'new India' of malls, coffee shops, pubs and clubs with an unusual stress on leisure. Urban centres now act as 'laboratories of style' – like the West End did centuries ago – where people go to observe and learn how to clothe and conduct themselves as 'competent moderns'.[10] Images are everywhere. We see through cameras – smartphone cameras, webcams, digicams (which got obsolete by the time I finished typing this sentence) – and read with a global visual vocabulary that comes to us through a gurgle of glossies, TV channels and the worldwide web. We find safety in pubs, lounge bars and indulgent departmental stores, more than on our roads. In a testimony to the power of the internet, Indian fashion bloggers get front row seats at fashion weeks. Using a proper noun to refer to a leather bag is de rigeur. Even I know about silhouettes and colour block – contrasting solid panels or blocks of colour, inspired by abstract art. In fact, we are almost on the verge of fashion fatigue.

From the traditional four main fashion weeks, there are now over a hundred fashion weeks held in the world across over 50 countries.[11] According to *Vogue* almost 30 important fashion weeks were scheduled through the year in 2016.[12] In India itself, the two main sponsors (Lakmé Fashion Week and Amazon India Fashion Week, the official fashion week in collaboration with FDCI) have at least two fashion weeks a year, each. In addition, there are a dozen more across the country. Just in 2016, Lakmé Fashion Week Mumbai showcased 92 designers and had 15 corporate sponsors, a 'new high'.[13]

Independent designers having found new iterations of the India-globe mix, excelled on the runway, yet the overwhelming influence of Bollywood prevailed more and more. Recently *Vogue* India celebrated the publication of its 100th issue. It was telling that of the 100, 76 issues had Bollywood related covers.

CHAPTER TWO

Faces of their Time

Meera, 1970s

I was maybe 16 or so. I won some Miss Photogenic contest. No, wait. First my grandmother made me join an *Eve's Weekly* contest, which I lost. Then, someone sent a picture of mine for another Miss Photogenic contest, which I won. And then Vimla Patil from *Femina* called up and said, why don't you join our pageant? Can you believe it? They used to call up people and request them to participate in Miss India!

I was doing my commerce (degree) at the time in Bombay, in one of the good colleges supposed to be for cerebral people. I belonged to a liberal Saraswat Brahmin family, so participating in the pageant was not looked upon as a taboo as such. But yes, in those days it was very different. Girls from 'good homes' never really went all out and did these things. So in a way it was pioneering.

We had nothing, zilch, no training for Miss India. We went on our own, had to do our own own make-up, wear our own shoes… National dress was your mother's sari, you know. The Miss India contest was a lot of fun but I just did it for a lark and went back to college the next day. After that I finished graduation, got married and had kids!

When we were [crowned] Miss Indias, we won things that would make us good homemakers, like sewing machines and fridges and irons. And a gold set, nominal cash – which of course, at that time, was a lot. I mean 5,000 rupees at that time was a lot of money! But today's girls are given job opportunities, they are given contracts, so that they can earn. They are given computers, things which can, you know, put them at par with men. At that time it wasn't like that. Here now they encourage you, earn your own money. That time they said, no, you stay at home and look after your husband, look after the home with your fridge and iron!

I'll tell you, at that time no one gave a hang about Miss Indias. Today I am getting more recognition for being an ex-Miss India than I did being a Miss India in that year.

Sometimes I feel…what if I had not married, what if I had joined the movies, what if I had done that…how would my life have been now? But of course, these are all the 'what-ifs'. Today's girls, if they join a contest and win it, they're not going to waste it. They're not going to get married and have kids at 22 like I did.

— ᴍ —

Shirin, early 1980s

When I started modelling I was 17. I was staying at a five star hotel in Delhi, when someone came up to me in the lobby and said, would you like to do this show? I said I can't, I have no modelling experience. Then they offered me a sum of money equivalent to a return trip to Europe, where my parents were. I was like, Wow! For one day? So I did it. I never thought of modelling as a career even while I was doing it, because I was studying alongside. To me it's always something I did on the side.

My first major work was the first Pragati Maidan show. It was in November, the textile Trade Fair show. I didn't have to learn anything or train. I worked for about six years and I did about 80 products. I did every TV and print ad. You would see me [selling] washing soap, you would see me washing my hair, brushing my teeth, wearing this saree, that fabric…so I was really the face of the time.

We had contracts for four years, five years. Once you signed that contract you had money coming in for four or five years – guaranteed. At 17 or 18, to earn 15-20 lakh per year is a lot of money, and that's 20 years ago!

I think we had the 'star status' that models don't get now because the star status is for Bollywood and cricket stars! We were glamour dolls, there's no question. Everybody was fair, good-looking and slightly exotic in a Western way. We were all 'Western-looking' girls and totally spoilt. I was the first model to be flown down back and forth from Delhi and when I landed anywhere for a shoot I had my own car, my own make-up person, my hairdresser, anything. Today, the girls can't even demand an air ticket if they're not big enough.

Today's girls are easily dispensable in this industry now…you can do two ads and nobody wants you this year. They'll say 'I'll get a new girl because new girls are cheaper, they are willing, there are so many of them.' In our times you had to beg someone to model! And even then they would whine, my mother says no, my husband says no, my boyfriend says no. Now with all these Miss Indias and the Miss Sunsilk and the Miss Ponds and so many Miss Whatevers, the ad agencies don't have to do anything. They can switch on the TV and choose from 20 girls at some contest.

You're slack, you've put on weight, you are not on time, you are sloppy, you have a foul temper – all these things can work against you very easily because somebody else immediately is ready to take your place. Whereas in our time, I could have the foulest temper but everybody would have to tolerate me simply because I was the face of that time. I was selling.

—⁓—

Niharika, late 1980s

I was in college in Bombay when the assistant of a well-known choreographer at the time, Jeannie Naoroji, came to my college, not headhunting but model-hunting. She saw me and sent a message through someone that she wanted to meet me for a show they were doing. I did one show and that led to other shows.

Initially I didn't take modelling so seriously. I come from a background where academics are a serious consideration. I was studying the social sciences and at 18, was confused about my career options. I wanted to be self-reliant and not depend on anyone for anything, but not by marrying rich.

My first job was a promotion of the shopping arcade at the new Oberoi hotel in Bombay. Although there were models like Anna Bredmeyer and Shyamolie Verma who were big names at the time, it wasn't publicized much. I got 500 rupees…which I had to give back! Because I was also trained by them, and that was the fees for the training! It wasn't much, but for me even 500 was a lot! Though we came from an affluent background, my parents tried to make us understand the value of money. I wasn't allowed to take the car to college. I was made to go by bus. So 500 rupees was a lot because it was my own.

The first show was just like that. She told me the basic choreography and that you have to walk straight, like you have a set of books on your head. So I did. Luckily, the first two-three shows were more like showings, so it got me a little more confident.

The turning point came early on in my career. Within four months or five months, I did a show for a Parisian designer and was offered a show in Paris. The reporters heard about it and wrote about me in a magazine's celebrity column. And then the same year, my friend and I won a competition in Europe where we had gone for a show. So two big things from international designers suddenly…you know how Indians are about international recognition! They all got excited about it, so my career took off.

Today's girls don't always understand the industry as a whole. Here, you meet a very wide spectrum of people. You meet people doing the ironing in the greenroom or the set workers. And you meet the high society people. I have conversations with everybody. But I know a lot of models now who don't even know what goes on behind a show. If you can open your mind, there's a lot you can learn from this industry. It's not superfluous as some may think. It's a proper industry that generates work for so many other people. Like any other industry.

—⁊⁊—

Ritu, early 1990s

I never really thought about entering the glamour industry until I was in Class 11. I don't think I even knew how to spell 'modelling'.

Then a friend from Chandigarh shifted to Delhi and she was aspiring to be a model. It was her dreams that I saw, and slowly the seeds were sown in me too. When I used to chaperone her on shoots, as everyone was wary about this business, one of the photographers suggested that I get my portfolio made and also give it a try. That's when I had some photographs clicked. They came out very bad; I didn't know how to pose or anything.

When school was finishing, I lost a grandparent who I was very close to. I managed the Board exams but could not get through any competitive exams. Then I got a call for a shoot from an old contact. I went against my family's wishes and insisted on doing the shoot. That's how it started.

When I mentioned the offer to my family there was a great deal of opposition. My family is very conservative. I was in a convent school, and led a very sheltered and protective life. I lived in a joint family. The only other woman in my family who worked was my aunt. She had a boutique, that too in the garage!

My mother was very vocal about her disapproval although my father did not say much. She burnt my portfolio to make her displeasure and disapproval more than clear. First there was the issue that no woman had ever worked in the family, then the profession itself. They had absolutely no good things to say about airhostesses or models or these kinds of professions.

But I insisted. See, the world is full of bad wolves, whichever profession you join, wherever you go, you only have to manage and protect yourself. I went straight from home and school into the working world. No college. I never did things like hang out with the guys in the canteen. And then one day I met my husband…

My first shoot was also the designer's first shoot. He had just passed out from NIFT. I did my first shoot for free. You don't get paid by designers anyway! Friendship is what I got from him. He did my trousseau, my Miss India clothes, he gave back in that way. My first proper pay was 1,500 rupees, which seems like a piddly amount, but for me it was amazing. With that I opened my own bank account; it was like setting up an independent life, something for yourself. It was a great feeling.

By the time I joined the Miss India pageant I was bored. I had done all kinds of work. *The Times of India* had called a couple of times asking me to take part in the pageant. The Miss India pageant is something permanent, the title stays with you forever. It was a different high from modelling. It made a difference to my career because I was able to raise my rate, get more money. Then there was extra stuff too, like inaugurating shops, cutting ribbons, the kind of stuff that comes with celebrityhood. Things change after you become Miss India, you are accompanied by bodyguards and everything.

My parents came to the contest, and I think I gained more trust and confidence from them after the pageant. Initially I was known as my father's daughter, but after my work and the title, he was known as his daughter's father.

In our time the body was secondary. What mattered more was your face. Today you can't say that any of them has a very pretty face. The industry has really come up; fashion is so BIG right now! I mean, you just have to throw a ball at a party and you will hit a model.

—⁓—

Pragati, mid 2000s

I started modelling for money, plain and simple. My father's family used to tell me that you can be a model, height *achhi hai*, but that was just in passing. They were not really serious. But I wanted to be a doctor or a scientist. I am very focused and once I set my eyes on a goal my eyes don't wander from the target. I was good in school, but despite my hunger to do well, I scored only 60 per cent in my exams. I was very disillusioned. My mother said, still you can do science and try for medicine. There was no money for me to pursue medicine. So I thought why not give modelling a try. I wanted to make money, not just for pocket money, but it was a difficult time for us.

I found one ad in the newspaper of an agency called Baja films. Without telling my parents, I took a friend and went to this agency in Connaught Place. There they told me, you have potential. You can register with us for 700 rupees and we will call you for some shoot. I was very happy because I had managed to save a little bit of money and that was just what I had. So I gave them the money, registered myself and came back. After some days I got a call from them, that there is a shoot at this address for some garment company, ladies clothes generally, and you just have to reach at this address, and you will get 1,500 rupees for it. This time I told my parents. They were not so happy, but there was little they could do. I went for the shoot, did it, and went back home.

I never even thought that they might not pay me for it. I was like a child, I just assumed that I have done some work for you, you will pay me for it. I was very innocent. When I called them later to ask about the payment, they told me 'we are not going to pay anything. It was your first shoot, we are giving you a break'. I was shocked but still I said ok, let me try other contacts. The make up person from that shoot gave me the contact of a photographer who took pictures of me and gave me suggestions about where I could go to distribute the photos for work.

In spite of doing the rounds, giving my photos, I did not get work. I think I was very homely in the way I dressed at the time. I used to just go for an audition dressed simply, with my hair just like a child's. The first time I went for an audition they de-selected me immediately. They saw me and said, no she will not do, maybe because they wanted a mature woman. I was very disappointed.

By now it was very frustrating because I was not making money, I was feeling that I am only putting in whatever little money I can, even to travel to auditions and make photos – it was very difficult. But when I woke up in the morning I would think, no, let me give it one more try, maybe something will happen.

Then I started entering these contests and got some award in a small local contest. Someone sent me to another photographer to click a proper photo. After this I got my first show thanks to a choreographer, for a designer in a farm in Chhatarpur. I got 3,000 rupees for it.

Then I heard of an international agency which had come to India, and that they have very clear fundas, no complications. They sponsored my being in their grooming course and gave me a one-year contract. Now it is eight months since I am with the agency and my life has changed. Since I joined, I have got a lot of work. I even went abroad for the Model Look of the Year contest representing India.

My rates are fixed by the agency. Before them, I never really had a rate as such, I'd do whatever work was given to me at whatever money was offered. I have just joined a gym and I have started getting conscious and careful of each thing that I eat. Because if I am doing this, I have to be number one. The number one international model.

I am a completely different person now. I used to be such a shy introvert girl that my father said that this profession is not for a girl like her. But I am a very adaptable person. And determined. If I have to be like this, okay I will be like this. I used to look very different also, I did not know how to wear clothes, maaro style and all that. Nothing. I was a child. Slowly I learnt everything. How to talk to people, and what people mean when they say certain things. How to be aware of your surroundings, how to manage things, how to understand people. I learnt it all.

DREAMS

From small small towns
From empty afternoons filled with boredom
Here we go my bag of belongings and I

The rain here is only a drizzle the rivers sluggish
From small tributaries here we go
Into the sea

The mighty train spews its smoke
Blows its whistle
Oh how it beckons me…

from 'Bunty aur Babli', 2005
Original Hindi lyrics by Gulzar
Translation by author

CHAPTER THREE

Almost Beauty Queens

Kamal is perhaps the tallest Indian woman I have ever seen.

'Miss India happened to me by chance,' she begins. Oh no, I think. Another by chance story, the building bricks of this industry. 'By chance' usually means that no one related to her was in the business, and/or that there was someone else complicit in the act – the one who posted the application or licked the stamps on the envelope. In Kamal's case, her friend had sent in her pictures to *Femina*, the women's magazine that organized the pageant.

Kamal, of androgynous name and androgynous frame, was the fifth of six sisters in a Marwari family from Rajasthan. They lived in Faridabad, an industrial satellite town about an hour from Delhi. Her father was a businessman, her mother a housewife. They were 'simple people'. Kamal's biggest obstacle was her mother, who said daughters from their family didn't go into fields like modelling. Kamal's efforts at convincing her did not succeed. Thanks to patriarchy though, if her father didn't forbid it, it was all right. Her father and sisters came to watch the pageant, but her mother stayed home in a final attempt to express disapproval. 'My dad was too happy. That moment I can't forget for the rest of my life. I was holding second position till the second last round.'

'Second position till the second last round' is not winning, though.

'Disappointment is always there,' she is nonchalant, biting into a chicken panini. 'According to me I feel I am a winner. Because what I went through nobody else went through. What with my family being against, this being against, that being against… too much stresshandle.' What else other than family was against her? Her words are a rap on my knuckles. 'Family is (enough)… what do you think family doesn't mean? Family is too much! I think people are blessed to have family support from the very beginning!'

As she launches into the rigorous daily routine charted out for the finalists of the Miss India pageant, I remember Honey's words.

Honey was a top ramp model at the time, some would even say the best in India. But in 1994, Honey had been a forgotten contestant at the Miss Indias. 'I learnt a lot from the Miss India process,' conceded the serious, straight-talking Honey to me, 'But they made us work so hard in the training period that I could not stand by the end of it. On the final day, I was so exhausted on stage that I thought I would fall any moment. They really shouldn't make the girls work so hard. It is too much.'

Kamal is more forgiving. 'I used to cry every morning thinking, oh my god what am I doing here! We had to run in the field and work out early every morning. Get ready in five minutes, have breakfast and be downstairs because your classes start at eight.' Classes on speech, deportment, general knowledge, make up, the science of beautification including cosmetic surgery, and question-and-answer practice that segue into Art of Living meditation classes in the evening, until a sparing dinner – sometimes followed by extra classes.

No cellphones, contact with family or boyfriends, and certainly no going out. With complete round-the-clock monitoring ('chaperoning') and strategic interventions to sculpt their bodies and minds into the Miss India moulds, the hope was that a perfect batch of Miss Indias would come out steaming from the ovens of the *Femina* kitchen. Money was riding on it.

'But I think that's how it should be!' Kamal reproaches me, catching on to my alarm, 'School is where you learn, isn't it?'

This school was in a five star hotel where the entire economy of the hotel adjusted itself to meet their demands. 'We had a separate diet for the *Femina* Miss India girls.' By this, Kamal doesn't just mean a separate buffet spread, but customized portions and diets for each contestant whose bodies had been scrutinized and lain inside a 'fat analysis machine' to scan the fat content. 'They told me that overall toning was required in my body. Because when fat analysis was done for all of us, mine was second last. That means I had the second lowest fat. But I had to tone up.' Kamal hastens to add that there were momentary lapses of reason, some midnight parties, a party being '...where you can eat anything.'

At any rate, a shot at the Miss India crown only meant one thing to her: a qualification.

Even being 'second position till the second last round' was a badge of honour for Kamal. She had graduated in the industry's eyes from the Ivy League of institutionalized pageantry. No May Queen amateur or Gladrags runner up ('People from Gladrags go to the Miss Indias, the Miss Indias never go to the Gladrags.') was she; she had acquired the requisite pedigree, and with 'Believe In Yourself' being her newly learnt mantra, she got to work immediately in using her qualification before she became stale as 'last year's batch'.

'I came back to Delhi, contacted few choreographers, coordinators... I think if you just have the *Femina* stamp it doesn't work. Until and unless you help yourself, nobody helps you...by then I knew this is what I love doing... I loved to walk the ramp, I enjoyed it.' She came back to a different Faridabad. The suburban town once dry enough to her to spark a forest fire was now a flood of fawning invitations to cut ribbons at local beauty parlours from aunties who had once looked down at her and bristled with indignation at her 'shamelessness'. Kamal says, 'When I came back, people who were against my going came to meet me. They are happy their name is associated with me.'

—⚬—

Twenty one, just returned from Toronto after a degree in business administration, Heerina came from a Sikh family from Delhi, where the tall, strapping women of the family with their skin like freshly churned butter, cheekbones like royalty and hair shining with amla-reetha-shikakai were naturally inclined for beauty pageantry. Her mother and aunts had given it a shot in the sixties and seventies, without luck. Instead, they married well, top class men, garment exporters with their own houses on refugee-claimed land in South Delhi.

Heerina's mother took Heerina, her peaches-and-cream complexioned first born, to baby shows as soon as she had spotted the potential, the child even winning a baby crown. She sent her to an international school and then college in Canada where many of her family members lived. Within months of her coming back, she decided that The Moment had arrived: it was time to send Heerina's application to the biggest baby show of all, Miss India.

Heerina resisted at first, slightly flattered, knowing that this had been on the cards, having done some modelling when she was 16 for a teen magazine. 'I don't think I'm that great,' she said to her mother, 'If you give me another year I'll be more confident about myself and deliver better.' No, no, no, her mother said. No harm in trying. At the most what will happen, she asked, pushing another parantha onto her plate, they will reject you? So what. We will try again next year.

Heerina was selected as a finalist. 'They must have seen something,' she shrugs.

'It's like clearing an IAS exam, and competing with the best of the best.' Heerina is ready with numbers. 'Last year there were 6,000 applications all over India. Of which only 29 girls were selected. Of which one girl did not turn up. So we were left with 28.' So you are the chosen ones from *six thousand* girls.'

This feeling of joining a historically ordained set of beautiful people kept up Heerina's morale through the training. This was what she told herself every morning when she had to wake up at 6 am and every night when she finally flopped, exhausted, often still hungry, on her bed at 11.30 pm.

The fat analysis machine had been replaced by an army of personnel from VLCC, a weight-loss brand. 'Everybody was analysed by VLCC the specific areas on which you should be concentrating and what your body requires, what you really need. They took everybody's body measurements, your height, weight so that you're not lying about it.'

Like in boarding school novels, the girls still managed to create an alternate universe of midnight snacking, furtive calls from hidden phones to boyfriends, smoking in each other's rooms, forming their own 'groups', disbanding their own 'groups', strung together by a feeling of being the chosen ones. Stories were told and retold amongst the contestants about how lucky they were, how they were still having it good, how the previous batch or the one before had had an even tougher time.

They preferred to think of the constant critical attention to food and deportment not as censure but in gentler terms: as care, as special attention, because that was the heady message thrown their way by the organizers. Because you were special, you had potential and you needed it; it was for your own good. Chaperones were appointed, ostensibly to look after the small needs of the contestants, help with baggage or dressing up, and little fetch-and-carry operations – but actually to keep watch on them.

This does not appear to Heerina to be a bad thing. This is what sets the Miss India pedigree apart from the other many 'body show contests'. Miss India isn't so much about the clothes, the bikini, the whatever. 'It's about class.'

'I went for Miss India in jeans and a top,' remembers Heerina. 'You can't just come and sit and say hi, hello (slumping and slouching to demonstrate) can't do that…have to be like (poised). It's something you need to learn, you can't just be faking it. Bit like table manners. There are seven forks and spoons in a meal… I mean I've never known this ever in my life…I knew there was a seven course meal but…fork, knife, half plate, soup plate, and when soup is about to finish you tilt it the other way and have it like this (demonstrating with mime). If you go internationally nobody will tell you there. You won't have a helper there. You're on your own at 22 or 23. They are just preparing you for the worst, or best, I would say. Today I know. I'm confident. If somebody tells me how will you have a seven course meal – I know.'

—៣—

A seven course meal is not on the agenda of the Gladrags contest. They are not looking for men and women to be able to delight a sick child or brunch with royalty. They are looking to do business.

Swati and Gurpreet filled up their Gladrags contest form in the early 2000s, about a year after they joined the modelling circuit. Not having been 'spotted' by an influential photographer or designer and swept up as their muse, they realized a year into their struggle, that 'a title was a must'. Swati got rejected for an assignment because she didn't have a title, while Gurpreet was consistently given the nose down treatment from her seniors. Both realized they needed some external help in stepping up their careers. Miss India seemed a little far-fetched and inappropriate given that what they really wanted was a career as a model, not as a beauty queen. They wanted more work, a different profile of work, and a price hike – not a year of social duties.

Swati and Gurpreet were both from middle class backgrounds outside the magnetic field of the fashionable set. Gurpreet's father was an exporter of electrical goods while her mother ran a local beauty parlour from their West Delhi home in a predominantly Sikh neighbourhood. Her older sister – a school teacher – was actually the family beauty, a typical Sardarni, she says, a little like Poonam Dhillon, equating her to the Bollywood heroine of the 1970s. Gurpreet had been the tall tomboy of the family, who had gone to a South Delhi women's college for her graduation in English Honours, and found herself becoming more feminine to fit in with her college mates. After being asked to compere a few variety shows by event management companies scouting the college, Gurpreet was asked by them to join the ramp events they were handling, 'because of her height'. Gurpreet realized there was something there, and as the ramp shows kept coming, she built her own skills, widened her networks with the make-up artists, choreographers and photographers, and prepared to get her folio done to make her next move.

'I used to watch FashionTV like till 2 am,' she tells me of her 'self training', 'See their walk, practise their expressions in front of the mirror or used to buy all these *Vogues* and practice their body language before a shoot. The next day I'd do that in front of the

camera and the photographer would say Whoa! What was that!…
Modelling came as something which I was always looking for. It
was so interesting. It was never for the money. In the beginning,
maybe I did give importance to the money but I never thought it
would be my career. After Gladrags I thought that yes, this is my
career definitely.'

Swati had tried her hand at different careers before turning to
modelling. She was from the Jat community, and her working class
father, mother and younger sister lived in a middle class colony in
South Delhi. Swati had been based in South East Asia, working as
an airhostess after graduating in hotel management when things
took a turn. She had been doing the Madras sector of her airline
and in her strolley every time she brought back business cards of
film directors and producers from South India who wanted to cast
her in their 'Southie films' and ads. After a few months, bored with
the monotony of mid-air clearing of trays, she quit.

Returning home to her parents, she started looking for something
more creative: she joined a design course at a local institute and
got a job with a prominent brand. Meanwhile, the business cards
from her airborne days beckoned and she reckoned, why not give
it a shot. Her always supportive mother found out about a well-
known fashion photographer who lived a stone's throw away from
their house, and walked down to meet him and tell him about her
daughter. Swati met him soon after, and taking one look at her,
the photographer nodded his blessings, and agreed to do a folio
for her – but only after she worked on herself. Her face was sweet
and pretty but with too much 'baby fat', he rued. 'Run, jog, lose it
all – get toned!' he told her, 'And watch fTV!'

So Swati, buoyed by her mother's confidence that it would
all work out, took up a gym membership and sweated it out for
45 days and changed her diet as advised by her trainer before
getting in front of the camera. With her mint fresh folio, she did
the rounds of the list of contacts the photographer had handed
her along with it. On the second day she landed a print ad for a
major brand.

Gurpreet and Swati were both Runners-up at their respective
Gladrags contests. Gurpreet says, 'I won Miss Photogenic also. I

knew everything about modelling when I went to Gladrags. I was already a one-year old model in Delhi… I was good but I was not being used because there is so much politics. After Gladrags it was just the hype which did so much to my career. I am loaded with work! I am doing campaigns, prints, ramp shows, everything.'

With her win as second Runner-up, Swati found people calling her for work – including those who had never returned her many calls, and had kept her waiting for days for a meeting. 'Getting the name through the contest really helped me increase my rates. Then I didn't have to approach people, people approached me. Of course with the contest I got to shoot for Bombay Dyeing which is the sponsor. For an entire year we shot for the magazine which really helped me in my career!'

Gladrags had a 'training' period too but unlike the Miss India training, much of the 25 days were photo-shoots, predominantly swimsuit shoots, television channel shoots, and choreography and practice for the actual show, rather than special classes. But for Swati and Gurpreet, this was what mattered, a juicy bite into the media circus that would leave a stain of a type of celebrity-hood. A stain like that of an exploded jamun fruit or a spillage of red wine, indelible for some time to come.

'I am a bit of a mini celebrity amongst my neighbours! Especially in my gym! And in the colony also. Recently a Hindi TV channel came to my colony gym to do an interview about my workout regime and all that, so now those who did not know also know about me…' says Gurpreet. 'You know before (Gladrags) it was like: Oh what is your daughter doing? Modelling. And what else? They said just modelling. That's her profession!?' The mimic in her comes alive and she puts on a shocked and preachy tone. 'Then they will say that it is not safe for a girl, no job security, late night, blah blah… I am from a Sikh family, so a huge family, relatives and everybody is so close-knit, even neighbours are close… But [after Gladrags] some of them were really nice. I went to my uncle's house yesterday for dinner. I am supporting my family and the money doesn't go to me or anything, I give it to my family, so my uncle is like hugging me and patting me on the back and saying that beta I am so proud of you.'

She shrugs. These are just words to her, likely to change with the weather. It isn't others' approval she is looking for, she assures me, reminding me about the car she bought for herself at the age of 20 with her modelling money. 'I am really happy I am working, I am earning. I am proud of myself even if nobody else is.'

CHAPTER FOUR

Two Worlds

BG Nagar is an island of affordability in an expensive South Delhi locality made of crowded gullies along which are stacked small rooms, one atop the other. Nancy lives on the ground floor in a two-room set partitioned away at the back of a bigger house. As soon as you enter, there is a recess in the wall that has been turned into a makeshift kitchen. On the left is a powder-blue fridge. The narrow sitting room has a folding cot, a cane sofa with muddy upholstery, a desk, a chrome and glass centre table and a large Samsung TV. On top of the TV is a box to keep pens and knick-knacks made by chopping the top off an empty cardboard box of Livon hair strengthening capsules.

On the walls are pictures of Nancy, alluding finally to her vocation. Between an oil painting of her done by her friend and a framed photo of her in front of India Gate is a classic portfolio shot – Nancy in full make up, a tight blue satin shirt and black pants against a soft lit orange background, hands on hips, hair billowing, head cocked towards the camera. Nancy shares the digs with her cousin. Both migrated to Delhi from Nagaland a few years ago, the cousin to study and Nancy to work. Nancy is a former Miss North East title winner, and an upcoming face in the modelling world.

The fan whirs over us slowly as Nancy brings me a glass of iced grape juice. She is wearing a loose black vest and a white pleated mini skirt. Every time I see a picture of Nancy in a magazine or on Page 3, I remember the whirring fan, the fizzy grape juice, the chopped Livon cardboard box. How different her real life was from these glossy images!

This disconnect remained through many interviews.

The sense of two different worlds peaked when the women I interviewed took out their black portfolios or files and spread out their photographs before me: here she would be aggressively pouting on the cover of a fashion magazine, there she would be a coy bride in a show exhibiting bridal wear. When we took our heads out of this sand of opulence, the drab and dreary upholstery of everyday life would greet us in the blue-tinged light. This contrast was small in comparison to the one that lay between many of the girls' real world back home and work world in the city.

—⁓—

Twenty-four year old Shivani came to Delhi from the 'holy city' of Benaras after graduation to pursue an MBA diploma. She didn't want to return home after completing the diploma, but her father, a wholesale trader of Benarasi sarees, wouldn't hear of her taking a job as it went against their caste norms. So instead, Shivani joined a three-month grooming course at the India franchisee of an international modelling and grooming agency. She explained to her family that it would enhance her personality and improve her marriage prospects. Her family agreed to shell out the 65,000 rupee fee for the course.

Instead of teaching household management or feminine social skills – which is what Shivani's family had assumed – the course focused on styling, ramp walking, and posing for photographs. In the 'graduation show' at the end of the course, Shivani won the Best Catwalk Award after which the model management section of the agency offered that she sign up with them, and try her hand at modelling. Shivani feared that her parents would immediately reject the offer, but she still decided to ask. They were shocked but grudgingly agreed that she could pursue it only as a hobby until her marriage was fixed with a suitable boy from the community. But permission came with a long list of restrictions. 'No videos, no movies, no serials. Print it's fine, ramp it's fine. Till the time you don't get married, you can do one or two assignments.' Shivani was relieved. 'Generally my community is very backward you know. They don't allow their daughters for the modelling thing.'

'One or two' turned into much more as Shivani found startling success, very quickly. International clients lapped up her dusky skin and exotic looks, and the agency found that it had a hot property in its hands. Didn't her list of restrictions hold her back from a full-blown shot at international fame and success? 'I am not that career oriented, only for time-pass I am in this line,' Shivani justifies to me, fiddling with the salad she is eating at the café in GKII where we are sitting. 'I don't wear anything revealing. My bookers never send me for such shoots. They know that Shivani won't do any shoot with bikini, or the cleavage showing or something like that. Because my parents are not like that. I myself don't have a problem wearing but ya, I like to maintain my own dignity, my family values, because they expect so much. They have given me this opportunity, that's a big thing… I am really obliged to them.'

I'm looking through her portfolio now and she takes it from me to flip to another page. It has a photo of her in a saree worn over what looks like…a bikini. She catches my drift. 'I did one or two shoots where I was forced to wear a bikini blouse, but I wore the coat or something over it, so it wasn't a real bikini shoot. It was within Indian clothes only. That's what I told parents. Parents were unhappy, but I'd already done it…'

The agency's director had lamented to me earlier, 'Shivani is so popular I can't begin to tell you. Every foreign agency that comes in wants to shoot with her. But her parents have different plans for her.'

Shivani says, 'My parents are looking for a guy. The day they find [one] I will leave modelling.' What about fame and fortune, I ask her, worried at this lack of ambition in her. What about what *you* want? 'That's what, I am not career oriented. Like they can find a guy tomorrow also, or maybe two months later. So I might leave in two days or two months. I feel somehow that love marriage doesn't go that well so I prefer arranged. I can wear only sarees after my marriage if my husband or in-laws say. I'll do modelling if they allow. If they don't allow, then I can help my husband in the business. That's it. So I don't have any high hopes or anything…'

'India is a male dominated society,' she says. 'It's a natural thing, that girls do the work inside the home, boys do the work outside the home. If I say to my mother "Bhaiyya can go out at midnight, why not me" she will say, "it's because you are a girl, you have to be back before dark. Because girls get raped not the boy."'

In my mind I bring together the arsenal I have to combat this understanding of the 'natural' order of things but she is not convinced.

'I know that I should know what to do, what not to do as a girl, should know household things… Because men don't have to do it. If woman doesn't do, then maids do.' I can't argue with the reality of that in India.

Shivani says that she is quite religious but doesn't keep a fast like many do in her home town, except for one – the 'Shivratri fast', a fast for Shiva, the patron saint of her town. And also the fast young virgins keep to find a good husband. 'Because my mom has said that you are staying alone there, don't fast. Of course after marriage, you have to do. Fasts for karvachauth, we have teej also…adi teej, chhoti teej, Ganesh chauth…not much.' Sounds much to me, I joke, and she smiles: 'In Benaras it would be nothing.'

Tell me about Benaras, I say, what is an old city like for young people like you?

'This world is very different from life in Benaras. Not a single eating joint, no good hall, nothing… there is only family, my house, my dad's shop, my few friends, that's it. It's a very slow life…but a very luxurious life. I don't have a car here, you don't have your parents, you don't have good food…here it's not that easy life. When I go back to Benaras I dress differently. I wear salwar kameez because my dad says whenever you come to the shop, wear suit, because you have the Muslim karigars and all.' What about your friends, I ask? She laughs. 'My friends there say that we cannot believe that you are a model! Whenever they see a magazine or something, they call me up and say…we have seen you again.' She looks down, modest but proud.

Shivani's sister-in-law also came to Delhi to do a month long course at another 'academy' in which she learnt table decoration and general grooming. This knowledge is not generally used in Benaras, Shivani acknowledges, but the exposure to the world outside is good for women, she adds. Shivani's friends and relatives back home often ask her to teach them about make up. In the eyes of her friends and family, her living in Delhi and her profession makes her emblematic of all the knowledge in this globalized world.

Shivani lives a compartmentalized life: modifying her behaviour, dress code, attitude, between the demands of international clientele, the life of a single woman living in paying-guest accommodation in Delhi, a good homely girl in Benaras and a highly rated professional model at Delhi's top modelling agency (their golden goose, in fact). The expectations from her as a woman, as a good daughter, appear to her to be written in stone, non-negotiable and normal in her community. Her stint in modelling is only a hiatus granted to her, a privilege revoked once a suitable boy is found.

Like a good daughter, Shivani sends all cheques home. Her family deposits them in her account in Benaras and she withdraws whatever she needs from the ATM in Delhi. Certainly, Shivani feels secure, safe and loved by her family and relatives. But what of the cost, I wonder? What of the threat lurking in the background if she deviates from The Plan? What of ambition? What of love? I am stopped in my thoughts when a voice filled with longing suddenly starts to sing a sad song from a recent Bollywood film, 'Agar tum mil jaao', the voice impassions, 'zamaana chhod denge hum…' 'If you become mine, I will leave this world for you.' It is Shivani's mobile phone's ringtone.

—⁂—

Nagaon is home to the one-horned rhinocerous and Kaziranga National Park along the banks of the once-blustering Brahmaputra river. Once a conglomerate of little kingdoms made up of big and small hills and seven rivers, a colonial administrator in the 1800s rearranged it on a map and called the newly organized settlement

'Nau gaon' or new settlement. Mayuri came to Delhi from a village in the Nagaon district of Assam. 'Telephone lines were laid here only five months back,' she claimed.

Mayuri was 'discovered' by an organizer of the North East Beauty Forum while she was going to school in a cycle rickshaw. She was in Class 11. The agent gave her his number and asked her to call him if she was interested in modelling. The dreams began immediately. Her first big journey was to the state capital Guwahati to participate in the Miss North East India contest, where she stayed for four days (she had never stayed overnight at the city before) at the contest venue ('for grooming, photoshoot, swimming'). After this experience, Mayuri dropped out of school, came to Delhi with a cousin who helped set her up in Lajpat Nagar and get some photos taken. She sourced the photographer and other contacts through Nancy, a previous winner of the Miss North East pageant, now slightly established as a model in Delhi.

Initially she had language problems as she did not speak English or Hindi fluently. The city – and being alone in the city – paralysed her. For two months she didn't leave the house to distribute the photos and get work. After managing to get work in two small ramp shows, she returned to Nagaon as she was too scared to live in the city. The next eight months were spent under a cloud of depression. Mayuri finally decided to come back and try again with renewed confidence. This time she returned alone. She decided that these barriers – of language, being from a village, and being alone – should not matter in the light of all she had read in the fashion magazines, and heard from TV and fashion circles.

In Mayuri's mind, there was not much difference between New Delhi and New York in relation to where she came from. As she says: 'I think for someone whose aim is to live in a city like New York or Paris, Delhi in your own country… it's nothing, nothing, nothing. When Gisele Bundchen came to New York she knew only Portuguese. Like this I found many examples. If they can do it, why can't I?'

By and by, Mayuri grew to enjoy the liberties of being without supervision. She began to work on herself with the aim of becoming an international success – joining English classes, equipping herself with a Rapidex Hindi-English reader in her handbag, taking salsa dance lessons and swimming classes to become freer with her body.

Before this she had joined a grooming course, although it did not work out the way she had hoped. She says, 'I joined MB Academy when I first came. There are two sessions – Group A is grooming, and Group B is modelling. I did not join modelling because I did not need to learn that. What I needed was grooming, to be polished and sophisticated. But the course had no effect on me. I just could not understand what people were saying. I could not express myself, I was too scared to talk. What I am learning now on my own has more effect.'

Mayuri recently went to Thailand on an assignment that she got through the internet. 'It's a very big assignment. My travelling, air ticket, everything was given by them. They received me at the airport also. Payment was ok… I am a newcomer so it was not so much. But for me what was important was that I got a foreign trip contract.'

Mayuri gets work to her liking in Delhi once in a while (although she is regularly offered C-grade music videos and other dubious assignments, which she rejects). Her career is not picking up at the moment, although she feels this is the time that she can utilize to learn and groom herself to be more 'modern' by learning English, salsa and swimming. 'I watch different TV channels, read international fashion magazines, see what is the latest fashion trend, which designer is doing what, which model is doing what… I learn which are the new mobile ring tones, about Hindi films, actors…where different countries are and so on.' She sees these as the valid knowledge in today's world that could help her climb the ladder. She is often subject to a particular kind of viciousness in the industry: intolerance for those disadvantaged with regard to English, modernity and urbanity. Many of her colleagues see her as someone who is 'out of place', 'trying too hard', 'desperate'. She says, 'Lot of my colleagues make fun…but my turn will also come. I am also watching them.'

Back home in Nagaon, things are very different. 'Baap re! East and West! I go home wearing salwar kameez. If I wear this (tight top, pants, heels, make-up) then I will become a roadshow, a nautanki! People there are very ignorant...they have no knowledge of fashion, they wear whatever – no matching chappal, bag, just like that. Now I tell them, wear this with that, match this with that. First I was like that only, but I came here, and learnt here, na? They are very curious about Delhi though. If I reach home late at night, then in the morning when I wake up there will be many small children gathered outside the gate to catch a glimpse of me. They keep sitting outside only! First time when I went back and people came to visit, we had to give them sweets – the ones that cost five rupees each? My brother after that has to now buy the sweets in kilograms.[14] I am a chhota-mota (small-time) celebrity there!'

Mayuri pauses to reflect. 'Whatever I am doing, I am doing with my own effort. Some of my relatives spend half their life getting a degree and still do not find jobs. Mujhe paap lagega (it's a sin)... me, without doing any studies only, in a city like Delhi, I am not asking for money from home for last few months. Maybe someday I will send money home instead.

For a girl like me, for my photo to come in *Delhi Times* or *HT City*, it's not a small thing. But I am not proud, not blind, not an ostrich. I can see I am getting less work and there are barriers. Still, I am young and I will learn. In Guwahati, there are so many like me, maybe more talented than me. But nobody had the courage to come here, try, struggle, all alone. I have matured all on my own.'

—◈—

Kavita was in Class 12 when she was crowned Miss Agra. Overnight, she became a local celebrity and the proud owner of 'a diamond ring, a wrist watch, a wall clock, a brass jug and mug' – the winner's loot. Soon after, she began compering at local shows and 'musical nites' where the director of an acting institute in Noida offered her a scholarship.

Not one to pass on opportunities, Kavita moved to Delhi once her 12th results were announced. At the three-month 'acting and presentation course' she met professionals from the industry including a fashion photographer. He took a set of photographs of her – her folio – and gave her a list of coordinators she could send the pictures to. Luck smiled and quickly Kavita started doing print shoots. 'Phir,' she says, 'meri gaadi chal padi.'

'For a good two years I only did print shoots until I met some choreographers, who became my friends and said "why don't you get into ramp modelling? Next time I do a show I would definitely take you". So I started doing ramp shows too. Side by side, I met few people who asked me "why don't you get into television anchoring?" And I started going for auditions. Then one make-up artiste told me her husband was a director. I met him and then I started doing cable TV programmes. Right now I am hosting a daily programme for one channel, a weekly lifestyle show for another and a programme about Page 3 parties in Delhi for a third.'

If it sounds easy enough, she is quick to add that it wasn't. Things didn't fall into her lap. She followed all possible leads through to the end, was disciplined and set herself a plan in an industry that she realized was haphazard and unstructured. 'I used to tell myself that every day without fail I am supposed to meet two or three new people. Whether it was a choreographer, designer, coordinator, or any journalist… I made an entire list and started calling people and meeting them. Whatever I did that time, a good six-seven months, that really helped,' says Kavita. 'It was very difficult, roaming around the whole city in so much heat, from one end to the other end of the city – having to look presentable also. But then I think one has to do that. You can't sit at home and think that work will come just like that. Not at all.'

Like a ship on its course, Kavita's career moved from port to port. I express surprise at how she missed docking at the Miss India and Gladrags contests, training grounds for so many of her peers. 'I did think of going for the Miss India contest, but dropped the idea once I began to get enough work without this "qualification". Gladrags made too much of wearing a bikini, which I did not want to do.'

Kavita consciously chose to work across sectors (ramp, print, TV) to outplay the vagaries inherent in modelling. She didn't want to leave her future to chance. 'Modelling is a short-lived career. Kitna hoga, five-six years, eight years? This was one reason I thought of getting into television, because television is something where there is no age limit. It works in the long term. I am busy throughout the month only because of this – either I have a fashion show, or a print shoot, or if not shoot, then my television work.'

She shakes her head as if correcting herself. 'Actually it is not that easy. One has to just really, really work hard to fill your time with some sort of work. I see girls who start modelling, work for six-seven months and then say we just can't do it, it is not happening. And they don't do it. I remember the girls who started modelling with me, now they are not doing anything, they have got married, they are doing some job, call centre, working in some airlines, whatever they got, and they stopped modelling.'

We are sitting at an Italian eatery in South Delhi, having worked our way through a four-cheese pizza. In her presence I have momentarily forgotten about the myth of flaky small town beauty queens; this here is no runaway with stars in her eyes. She is a businesswoman, a 23-year old entrepreneur whose words reflect her strategic assessment of the 'market'. Not for her, lofty dreams of dinner with Gisele Bundchen or passively outsourcing a career plan to an agency. Kavita has studied the local market, identified the segments where she can generate work and has strategically and systematically gone about doing it. She has a plan for every step, including her next: a move to the real tinsel town, Bombay.

She was reluctant so far to make the move because of inside talk of the unavoidable and all-pervasive casting couch in the Bombay film industry. To hedge this risk, she has hired the services of a 'PR girl' to distribute her showreel and generate a certain amount of work for her. She will wait a few months to see the response from Bombay – her eyes are on getting a lead role in a TV serial – and then take a final call on whether to move. If she does move, she also plans to enlist the help of an agency: 'I would not join an agency here in Delhi – why give them 30 per cent for work I am generating anyway myself? But maybe I will in Bombay. I don't know too many people in Bombay, so if I shift there and join an agency, initially it's going to be a great help.'

One thing is for sure. She's not going back to Agra. 'It is very different. Agra is a small city. What after you have done your graduation? There is nothing exactly happening there. Everybody knows each other so one has to be really, really careful. In Delhi girls and guys they can go out together, in Agra it is just an impossible thing. But then at the same time I feel being close to Delhi, it is not that backward also. People from Agra visit Delhi often.' Kavita gestures to herself and her outfit and shakes her head, 'I definitely can't wear this in Agra!' – a fitted sleeveless shirt with pants. 'I have to really think when I pack my stuff for Agra. I make sure I wear a top with sleeves, not too figure hugging or tight, no tummy showing, loose and basic make-up. I just tie my hair, khatam. I just carry one flat shoe, I go, finish my work and come back.'

Like unequal lovers though, Agra waits for her return. For this city, she is a celebrity, a carrier of the winds of the glamour world. Local newspapers keep track of her achievements. She is considered an 'expert' on the industry, and regularly asked for advice by those wanting to try their luck in the field. Kavita feels that others from her hometown may not be as lucky. 'You know I met lot of girls, they are very beautiful, but one thing is missing – what we call "class". Pretty looking girls with good figures but she studied in some chota-mota public school, probably Hindi medium, can't speak English properly. It then becomes very difficult to operate in Delhi, where everybody talks in English, and if you speak in Hindi they say, oh she is a ganwaar, a villager. I was from a convent, the best school in Agra, and it makes so much of a difference.'

Kavita is ambitious and unencumbered by the demands of tradition, or the expectations of her parents, although it isn't like she is untouched by these spectres. 'I am a Kashmiri and in my family I'm the first person who is into this field. Relatives indirectly tell my parents this work is not supposed to be clean and girls are not safe here.' Her businessman father and housewife mother have come to terms after four years with her independence, and quashed their dream of finding her a good Kashmiri Pandit groom.

Kavita is clear that she will no longer return to a small city: for her, the anonymity and cosmopolitan freedom in a metro is non negotiable, and she is willing to fight for it. 'My parents in the beginning were very tense about finding a match for me. My mom was too much into finding a Kashmiri but now…there aren't many guys whom my mom feels that I can stay with!' Has Delhi made such a difference? Her sisters are also in Delhi now, do they feel the same way? No. Although her sisters also live and work in a metro she doesn't think they are removed from tradition. What has made an impact, she feels, is her years in modelling. They have made her tough, as well as slightly suspect in the eyes of potential suitors looking for traditional wives – which works in her favour, she says cheekily, these are not the men she wants anyway.

With each little success, each cheque, each show, each alliance made independently, she saw herself change. 'Even inside,' she says alluding to her internal transformation – a rising confidence and self-worth that made her see her own life as a woman in another perspective. As a life filled with possibilities, that cannot, should not be clipped by 'small town values about marriage or morality' she has now outgrown. 'There is so much risk in arranged marriage anyway. What if after one month you realize you don't get along with that person? Then you have to stay with that person because the whole society knows that you have got married to that person? You can't divorce that person! When I look around I see, hazaaron log separate hote hain…if a marriage doesn't work out, better to separate and get divorced. Now I don't care about the world too much. Life is definitely more important.'

CHAPTER FIVE

The Fantasy Body

It takes me a while to get past an enduring myth.

Models aren't actually Xerox copies of one another.

They have different body types based on the kind of work they do. To stride on the ramp, they need those endless legs and a skinny body. Skin color, bust size and the face are not relevant. What is important, is 'attitude' and 'projection'; the ability to carry off all kinds of clothes. If they want to rule the print media, however, they cannot do without being fair, photogenic, and conventionally attractive.

To beam out of the TV screen, they must meet the requirements akin to a matrimonial ad: a pretty face, perfect smile, fair skin, medium height, slim, fitting the 'girl-next-door' brief. To sizzle on the big screen of Bollywood they need all that is needed for TV, and a little more: preferably on the chest.

What this means, to read the fine print, is that models have to change their body type if they want to do a different kind of work. Or, as Roopali found out, if they move location to work in another 'market'.

Roopali modelled part-time for a few years in Hong Kong, where she was stationed as an airhostess. She says, 'To be a model in Hong Kong I had to be really lean, because that's the norm in for Chinese people. They're really skinny – I'm considered bulky there, in fact. I had become skinny automatically because of the food habits there. Plus my work profile had heavy physical work. Being an airhostess, you look pretty and you work like a horse!'

She returned to India as a result of the SARS (Severe Acute Respiratory Syndrome) epidemic in 2003. When the crisis was declared over and expatriates given the option of returning to their jobs, Roopali decided to stay back in India and pursue modelling full time. She joined an international agency that had just opened its offices in India but faced a slight problem. 'When I came back, people used to consider me too skinny because Indian models are slightly different from the Hong Kong build. So I had to put on some weight and tone what I had by starting to work with weights. Only then did I start to get work here.'

What happens when a model wants to make a more drastic transition, from one kind of work to another, beyond just putting on or losing weight? Swati spent two years working hard on her 'natural body' – once losing weight and getting the correct body type to suit a Gladrags contest, and then again changing her 'Gladrags body' to gain weight and have dental surgery for a new 'TV body'. She planned to move to Bombay to try her luck at television serials and commercials. 'You need a different body type for that kind of work in Bombay. They don't care if you're fat or short…they just need that pretty presentable face. That lovely smile. And so I've got my smile corrected also.'

Swati went to a large private hospital in South Delhi with her mother to consult a dental surgeon. 'The doctor gets a lot of people coming in for this treatment. People from everywhere – those who are about to get married, airhostesses, people in the service industry, and models. At least 10 references she showed me. It's a very common treatment. All the Miss Indias get it done.'

What does the surgery actually involve, I ask her? Swati explains, 'They grind your original teeth about half way and then they cap it. It's a very expensive treatment…a lot of my savings went on it…but it's worth it.' It had sounded fairly simple to Swati. But what she didn't account for was the pain.

'The doctor didn't tell me it was going to be so painful!', she laughs, a little embarrassed. 'When I went for my first sitting, I realized it wasn't easy. They had to give me local anesthesia, and there was a lot of bleeding, lot of pain. I really suffered for a month. For three sittings she was just grinding my teeth. Meanwhile she gave me temporary caps, which looked horrible. I couldn't work while the caps were on. Neither could I go out and meet people.'

Didn't you have second thoughts, I ask? Pain could be a real deal breaker.

'I did,' she nodded, 'after the second sitting. But then it was halfway there! I couldn't go back on it. It was a bit too much, all this…bleeding and…it was horrible.' She shudders. 'Anything sweet just went and hit my gums so badly that the pain just lasted for two days, three days. But I managed… I took a lot of painkillers.'

The whole procedure took an excruciating month and a half. Swati was happy at the end of it, and thought the results were worth the pain. Except for one thing.

'Now for the rest of my life I can't bite into anything hard with my teeth. Like an apple. I have to slice everything and eat. The doctor had just told me as far as the apple goes! But I realized four months back that I could not bite into corn on the cob, my favourite. I called the dentist and said to her: You didn't tell me I couldn't have corn on the cob.'

—✺—

On my flight was a conspicuous duo. Two women, looking like mother and daughter, were going through the motions at the security check. The younger woman was tall, thin and fair and could very well have been a model, or aspiring to be one. She must have been around 18 or 20 at most. What was striking was the plaster on the young woman's face, arranged like a sign-off for a nose job. As mother and daughter donned their dark glasses, shutting out the world, I sat thinking of another young woman who'd shared her experience with me.

Mita was 19 and had joined an international modelling agency in Delhi, where she was advised to get a nose job. The agency felt she had tremendous potential – but for her nose. Mita told herself that there was no point in being in this industry if she didn't do it. 'Yes I was getting work,' she reasoned, 'But what's the point in getting money and not getting recognition?' She put aside her fears sternly, had a good cry after asking herself a hundred times: 'what if it goes wrong?' But in Mita's mind, if she wasn't willing to take the risk, she should just look for another career. These changes were mandatory, she imagined, in her chosen field.

She, along with her agent, was referred by those in the know to a doctor in Bombay: 'We didn't want to just do it with anyone, obviously it had to be someone who was an expert.' Mita, accompanied by her mother and her agent, went to Bombay to seek an appointment with the very busy doctor. Even Mita was surprised at how quick and business-like the first meeting was.

'We didn't have any telephonic conversations beforehand nor did he show me any references or pictures. I thought he would show me a computer image or something to show me what it would look like. But no such thing. He didn't even draw a diagram. He only explained it indicating it on my face. He refused to meet my agent, because she was not related to me. Only my mother and I met him. He said it's a regular operation, lots of people undertake it. He asked me to come to the hospital next morning at 9 am for the surgery.'

A difficult night, I wager? Mita laughs. 'That night I went partying. This was my way of dealing with it. My dad called and said, Good luck for the operation! And I was like, yeah ok. We didn't make it such a big deal.'

But it was, in fact, a fairly big deal.

'It was a one-hour operation. When I was lying on the stretcher before the operation, I was nervous. One male nurse came to me and asked, toh theek ho na? He told me, don't worry, local mein hoga na aapka operation. Local, I said? Basically they were going to numb my face, the area around my nose, and do the surgery, so I would be awake through the procedure! That psyched me out a bit. But once I was wheeled in, the doctor told me to just go to sleep. And I found myself being a bit drowsy and actually going off to sleep. They put an IV drip into my wrist. That was the only thing that hurt.'

Mita describes the procedure in some detail to me. 'They didn't really make any cuts on top of my nose...only two slits under both my nostrils which were stitched up later, and the stitches removed.

They inserted some equipment, they could see the inside on a monitor in front of them and drilled, chiseled away at the bone on the nose bridge and brought the cartilage at the sides in.

After the operation I could breathe only through my mouth for a while, and that was tough. There was pain, so I was having painkillers. They had inserted two gorges up my nostrils for one day or so, and after that a metal cover was placed on my nose for protection.

Immediately after the surgery yes I could see the blood, so it was a bit scary. Blood would drip down from the nostrils and I would have to keep wiping it off. But it was more psychological, I mean, that happens, but it's just the thought of blood that is a bit scary. I only saw my face after I got home.'

By home, Mita means home in Bombay, where she was staying with her distant cousins, who had been told about the procedure so they could provide moral support to Mita's mother. 'I think it was important for my mother that she be with people she knew, to have her own support. It was difficult for her, she was worried, crying a bit…but she was ok.'

Recovery was harder than Mita had expected. It took about a week for her to feel better. She could eat 'more or less anything' but found it difficult to speak 'as it was all connected, and mostly because of the tight bandages on the nose'. But the biggest problem was something else. 'My eyes were all bloodshot and the area under both my eyes became black and blue and yellow. It was like I had been boxed in the eyes. But apparently that happens if you do any kind of surgery to the face. The area around the eyes takes the trauma. It took more than a month for this to go, so I had to try and cover it up and put make up, or something or the other! The doctor had not told me about this!'

The anti-climax of it was that when Mita returned to Delhi with her new nose, people couldn't really tell. 'It was only in my pictures that you could make out the difference. And it did make a difference. Lots of people do it, but don't say it… I don't know why.'

There is another elephant in the room. The Size Zero one.

Anorexia popularly refers to an obsession with body image, particularly being thin, which manifests itself in the behaviour of (mostly) women and girls who either starve themselves for fear of putting on weight, or induce themselves to forcibly vomit or purge themselves after eating meals so that the act of eating itself does not affect their propensity to gain weight.

More explicitly, in connection to the fashion world, it is often attributed to the idolization of the stick-thin bodies of models that walk the ramp. Implicit in this is the assumption that models themselves are likely to be anorexic.

In the last decade there has been more public debate around it in India, with the word anorexia finding its way into the media. Despite it being a well-known term bandied about in the media in connection with models, there were many women in the modelling industry who did not know what the term meant. Some used the word 'anorexic' as a synonym of 'thin' to describe the preferred body type in the fashion industry, without realizing that it was a reference to a medical condition or an eating disorder. Pragati, who is with an international modelling agency for the last two years, talked about her encounter: 'I went to Shanghai for a contest representing India. There I saw the other foreign models were so skinny and so young! They were 13-14 years old, and did not eat the whole day. Some fainted also. Some would just starve themselves and vomit... I did not understand what it was. Anorexia? No I have never heard of anorexia... But these girls were so young it was shocking. In it there was a lesson for me. That you should not starve yourself.'

Some had noticed odd eating patterns in their everyday interactions with one another. Swati recalled, 'I've seen people who during shows, when we spend the full day together, they just don't eat.'

Only one case of medical anorexia was reported (of a third person) in one interview in which a young model underwent such a drastic weight loss that she was forced by the agency to quit modelling. However this was the only (and vague) incident that I heard about in the course of my interviews.

Veteran model Niharika suggested this is because of issues of scale. 'Here the industry is not large enough for something like this to get so rampant. So knowledge is low because there's no one who has been majorly anorexic or bulimic. You'll not get any models who have died of anorexia or touchwood have gone to that extreme a situation.'

'No one had died of anorexia yet', unlike the West. Couched in the language of problems with 'dieting' (a much favoured term in Indian vocabularies, especially of older generations who wonder if you're 'dieting' if you refuse the third rasgulla), anorexia is outside the imagination of the Indian mindset. Anorexia remains in perception as a Western problem that has not reached Indian shores – or at least the Indian modelling industry.

While loudly denying that anorexia exists in the Indian modelling scene, many agree that the misconceptions around being thin affect the younger generation today. This guilt – that the industry leads thousands of gullible young girls to starvation in pursuit of bodies similar to theirs – is a recurring feeling in interviews with better known models and choreographers. Niharika often comes across people who are trying to become thin, through any means possible.

'I met a waiter of a hotel whose daughter was 13 years old and wanted to be a model. He told me, she considers you a role model, I don't know what to do with her – she is dieting and she doesn't eat at all. She has been hospitalized once. I told him that I want to talk to her. Unfortunately she was not in the city at that time, so I told him. Please tell her, this is a personal message from me, to NOT do this. If she does this she is never going to make it because she is going to kill herself before that! And this is not what we advocate. And I say this at every interview, at every place I can to aspiring models. You can't go on a crash diet. Try and change your style of eating, eating healthier food and eating the right quantity, the right combinations, rather than doing irrational things!'

Vidyun, choreographer and godmother to many of the older generations of models seconds Niharika's claim that it is people outside the industry, young modelling aspirants, who are more susceptible. She says, 'Those who are aspiring to be models tend to take fairly drastic measures. And I am saying this from experience. I was a judge in one of these regional competitions (for a model hunt), and I do remember being alarmed – and I am reusing the word alarmed – because at the end of that, when I was waiting for my car outside, somebody who did not make it through to the next round came up to me with her mother. She was weeping and saying I want to know why I was not selected.

And I said, listen, we can only take 10 or 20 out of a 100, so… Then she said, "But I haven't eaten a square meal in one year! I have been so passionate about this as my profession! What don't you like about me?" I was getting quite psyched by the entire thing, because… I mean, I didn't even know which number she may have been as part of the competition! But she continued saying, "If you think my nose needs to be redone I can get a plastic surgery done." Now that's very very desperate which could lead to severe disorders, to health problems, to mental self esteem problems. I'm afraid it does happen.'

But can you blame it on the models? Vinita, a senior model, echoed several of her colleagues when she said, 'You can't stop the media, you cannot stop TV. At 12 you have what, parents and teachers? Everybody wants to be a rock star, a singer, an actress, a model. It's a child's dream. But it's up to the parents to guide them sensibly.'

Perhaps we need to look elsewhere to find where to place 'the blame', several suggested. We live in a world with abundant food choices, a lifestyle that encourages eating out, socializing in restaurants and coffee shops. The same world gives importance to being slim and idealizes and rewards thin women. Perhaps anorexia is an outcome of these contradictions that globalized culture creates in a young urban population, especially women?

In 2006 the organizers of Madrid Fashion Week banned underweight models from participating. They ruled that no models with a Body Mass Index (BMI, ratio between height and weight) below the standard 18 were permitted to walk on the ramp, as they contributed to an unhealthy body image. This made the headlines in Indian media but models maintained a discreet silence. What emerged again was the opinion that such a ruling did not affect India. The incident led me to calculate the BMI of the women I interviewed, based on the heights and weights they had claimed to be. All those who reported their heights and weights (20 out of the 30 women I interviewed) – assuming that they had given their correct heights and weights – were underweight, as per international standards. Not one person made the lower limit of the normal weight BMI range, that is, 18.5.

—◊—

Mita did indeed get much more work after the nose job. She became the agency's top model and went on to win the Miss India title. In an interview (as the new Miss India) on a TV chat show, where the host enquired about using such new techniques, Mita made no mention of the nose job she had undertaken a year back, but confessed to having undergone gum surgery to fix her smile. She explained that when she saw the videos of herself winning the crown, she realized she had a flaw – a 'nervous smile'. In the throes of the post-win analysis, she went through a minor gum surgery, which she hoped would steady her smile, and increase her chances of winning at the international level.

The host applauded her honesty and herself admitted to having taken a few Botox shots to smoothen the lines on her forehead, having previously alluded to Botox as 'a lunchtime procedure', 'a magic wand'. In the conversation that followed they echoed the overall refrain that cosmetic surgery is a matter of 'choice', it is a 'right' like any other, and we were lucky that we had the opportunity to avail of such advances in technology.

Increasingly, there is a sense that appearances are everything. And not just in modelling, as a senior model, Naina, pointed out: 'It's in all professions. As a generation, and as a country we are now becoming really obsessed with the way we look. And it's true. You do get certain advantages if you look a certain way.' People feel that physical appearance and a glamorous image will widen economic, career and social opportunities and facilitate social mobility.

An urban legend goes like this: industrialist Anil Ambani, in his plump days, was once told by a foreign client that 'if you can't take

care of your own body, how will you take care of our business?'
The question pushed him to begin a punishing regime to look fit
and suitably lean and mean, to show the world that he embodied
a fit, thriving, healthy business.

Like ballet dancers or boxers, women engaged in modelling
and glamour related work have to take special care of their bodies,
and achieve a certain body type to match the needs of their work.
The gym becomes more than a building, a room equipped with
weights and other equipment or a facility to exercise, it becomes
a social universe of its own – a social and professional space
which sets the normative standards – of bodies, of the time
and efforts that others in the profession are putting in, thereby
setting reference points for one another. And an important place
to network, exchange information and conduct business, and in
a way carry out – in body work sociologist Carol Wolkowitz's
words – 'employment's numbing routines'.[15]

Do models think more about their bodies than ballet dancers or
boxers? Does it have more of an impact on their personal lifestyles
or mental make-up? It is difficult to say without falling into a
swamp of prejudices, given that there is scant evidence out there
of what it means to do 'body work' – the host of occupations that
depend on the body in a more organic, intimate way. 'If you gain
three kilos you could be out of business for a week.' Namya, the
producer of Channel V's Get Gorgeous model hunt had realized
after getting a glimpse into what working on your body as a model
really meant.

The credit for creating these sculpted bodies is often not given
to the persons themselves but to the experts who claim to have
'manufactured' it. A massive life-size hoarding outside a posh gym
in Bombay once showed a young model who was to be (at the
time) featured in a Bollywood film showing off his toned torso and
spectacular abs and pecs. The text above the picture read 'Upen
Patel…. By Sykes' (the name of the gym), implying that the body
on display was made by the gym and not hard work by the model
himself.

There is a tendency to automatically assume that women in
the industry suffer complexes of body image. But carrying out the

rituals of body work – going to the gym or parlour or keeping to a diet – is different from the low self esteem and anxiety associated with the politics of body image. The lines are blurred because what is being 'worked on' is the body itself, an intimate part of personhood that it is difficult to be objective about. So to ask where work ends and vanity begins, or where professional necessity is overtaken by personal indulgence is unlikely to yield easy answers.

There is a link however between the model's disciplined routine of maintaining a certain body type, and its contribution to the creation of a norm.

From corsets in the 19th century to high heels today, there have been a range of disciplinary practices which have served to define 'femininity'. Simone de Beauvoir wrote of the astonishing breadth: 'Chinese women with bound feet could scarcely walk, the polished fingernails of the Hollywood star deprive her of her hands; high heels, corsets, panniers, farthingales, crinolines were intended less to accentuate the curves of the feminine body than to augment its incapacity.'[16]

Women in the glamour industry adopt these disciplinary practices as tools of their trade, but are also implicated in creating a norm and defining femininity. The problem is that these norms are then used to evaluate and control us, and exclude those who do not conform.

Being fat/short/dark is alluded to as a problem in popular media and solutions are simultaneously offered. Surgical procedures are advertised in every neighbourhood, on street buntings, outside the local beauty parlour, in the leaflets that fall out of the daily newspaper, on the back of magazine covers lying on the table in the dentist's waiting room. New products – creams, lotions, hair-dye, serums, gels, vitamins – from competing brands promise to provide an 'anti-ageing solution' and embalm you in a timeless vacuum. In a twisted real life incident, newspapers reported a shocking case of a young girl in Delhi who killed herself because she felt she was too fat.[17] The incident brought out various other reports by counselors in schools who shared their concerns about the mental trauma that they were witnessing overweight and not conventionally good-looking children go through.[18]

A controversial advertisement for a fairness cream exemplifies this: it shows a young woman dreaming of being a sports commentator on television, yet being unable to because of her washed out personality – a euphemism for her dark complexion. Following advice from a kindly soul, she turns to the fairness cream and within two weeks has turned into a radiant fair beauty. As a result she is picked up by a TV channel and becomes their star commentator. The message is this: only if you conform to these standards of femininity can you succeed.

—⁓—

Fashion is fickle. Any seasoned model will tell you that the most desirable body type is a moving goalpost. Niharika ruled the ramp in the 1980s but never got print ads because she was 'dark, tall and had hair which nobody knew how to handle'. In Niharika's time, her dark skin may have been a no-no but in many cases today, being 'too fair' is a disadvantage.

Shivani's dusky skin is what kept her in high demand from international clients. Her agency is delighted that her skin colour sells so well in the global market. If only, her agency feels, she was thinner (than the 50 kilos Shivani weighs), she would be a perfect confluence of desired traits of the East and West – dusky, exotic and skinny.

Tina feels that she is discriminated against in the industry sometimes because she's 'too fair'. She says, 'Now with all this bronzed look and everything there are certain photographers who keep going on and on about dark beauties, and you are completely sidelined.' Tina decided she had to act on this. 'I always have to wear a body tan because people get startled when they see how white I am. See this is my real skin colour...' Saying this, she raised the bottom of her pants to reveal an ankle with her real skin tone – completely different from the rest of the skin that was on show. She had applied a colouring agent on all parts of the body that would show – her face, neck, arms. 'I have to always have this tan make up on. Even my agents demand that I get ready like this when I come for auditions or meet clients.'

The scales keep sliding, responding at the slightest touch to global market pressures and the whims of successful designers. Some decades the preferences tilt towards the dusky. Some designers prefer fuller models in particular years. Some markets like very Indian features, while others prefer a 'global face'. In just two decades, there have been striking changes in the ideal Bollywood heroine. A phase went by in which having a 'good body' was suddenly very important, sending even the laziest of actors and actresses into gyms to get a sculpted and toned body. Fantasy bodies change. The bikini-body for women, the six pack abs for men are new developments in the history of what constitutes a desirable body. Even for men, the ideal has changed. From the muscled and oiled Arnold Schwarzenegger wide tapering torsos to the current ideal – a taut and lean body, sporting a beard and a man-bun.

Everybody fantasizes about the body they could have, a departure from the one they really do have. For a model, there is no scope for this duality between the fantasized body and the real body – her real body *is* the fantasized body, and the everyday struggle is to maintain this convergence. The irony, of course, is that this convergence never really materializes.

Even as her real body is the fantasy of another's, she is chasing another, shifting ideal of the fantasized body.

FIELD

What really distinguishes ethnography from other interview-based methods is the full scale immersion in a community. We do what I sometimes call, simply "deep hanging out". Or as my writer-husband sometimes affectionately calls it, "gossip with footnotes".

Alma Gottlieb, *Cultural Anthropology*, 2016[19]

CHAPTER SIX

A Feminist at Fashion Week

The preoccupation with labels is the first thing I noticed as I stepped into the Lakmé India Fashion Week in 2004 at the Grand Hyatt hotel in South Delhi. Are you a delegate? Are you a buyer? Are you a designer or a model – that too, chosen by the select panel of organizers to work in the shows? Are you 'press'? Only a yes to these questions will win you that coveted delegate card you can hang around your neck, a neckpiece so precious it could be studded with jewels. Even with this, a select few get to go anywhere, anytime. As two unlikely attendees slink past, I catch the labels round their neck clearly proclaiming them to be 'contractor' and 'casual labour'. Only a determined mind can crack this wall and slip past stone-faced men in uniform or smartly dressed young people chewing gum and armed with walky-talkies – employees of the event management company tasked with keeping the circle of style from being infected by unfashionable masses and the occasional nosey PhD student.

It was my first foray into fieldwork. Fashion Week seemed like a logical place to begin, a fixed time in a fixed location when disparate members of the industry came together in some cohesiveness that came closest to the traditional concept of the 'field' and gave a sense of who was the 'community'.

I was here on a mission: to observe what the field of fashion was like and find women models who would agree to be interviewed as part of my research and let me in to their lives. I had loftier goals too. To squirrel my way backstage and observe from the inside.

By the end of the first day, I realized how naïve the goal was. A systematic trail of hurdles had to be crossed to gain entry to any part of Fashion Week, forget backstage. A combination of keys would give me access to the three main front areas: the buyer area populated with stalls of designers where business was to be conducted (for which I needed a delegate pass); the seminar hall where panel discussions on the Business of Fashion were to take place (for which I needed a seminar pass); and the show area where over 40 fashion shows had been scheduled for the week (for which I would need a separate pass for each show I wanted to attend). I had with me only two seminar passes (my two aces, it turned out) that the organizers had given me as consolation after refusing me a general pass. I had awkwardly asked a classmate, a prominent fashion designer's son, to get me entry backstage but he refused, citing a dragon choreographer who had breathed fire at the suggestion of my alien presence.

Inherent slips in design though made some trespassing possible. The first was to host it in a five star hotel, the lobby of which is never fully private. If you couldn't access the shows, you could at least access the people going into or coming out of the shows. That year, designers had been given suites on higher floors of the hotel to show their wares and conduct business with buyers. If you could camouflage yourself as a visitor staying at the hotel, you could go up to the suites.

Having finished with a recce of the open access areas and some elevator trespassing, I wandered the hotel lobby wondering what to try next when I bumped (literally) into a college friend's husband. 'What are *you* doing here?' he asked, as if I was the most unfashionable person on earth. He, though no sapeur himself, was in the employ of one of the major sponsors of the event. On hearing my despair, he handed me my third ace: a special VIP pass to the opening designer show of the week.

My special VIP pass meant that, one, I could sail through three layers of security without questions, and two, I didn't have to go in through the plebeian door where media-types waited in a pile like hungry wolves to rush in once the doors were opened. I bypassed this mass of hot breath and cameras and tangled wires and glided into a separate area cordoned off by silk rope where men who looked like bouncers at a nightclub smiled uncertainly at me. It also meant I could choose to sit where I wanted in the first two rows. A bit worried that the first row was too close to the ramp, I opted for the second, the politics of Front Row seating escaping me at the time.

The Show Area was the centrepiece of LIFW, security escalating as you got closer to the final door leading into what was essentially a large banquet hall. In the hall, a long ramp had been constructed and seating set up for an audience of about 250 people in step formation, with chairs fitted with white cloth sheets as if caterers had been let loose before a wedding. A whole wing was reserved for the press. While audiences sat on both sides of the ramp, right in front, a little distance from where the ramp ended, was a marked rectangle: the reserved space for the cameras and flashlights. Photographers and camerapersons with heavy equipment climbed over each other to get their shots, making a craggy black mountain in silhouette once the lights dimmed.

The show starting the Week was expected to be, trade papers had whispered, 'bold'. The designer whose show it was (Rina Dhaka) apparently had a reputation for being, well, 'bold' because of her sensual designs. I assumed this to mean there would be some sexy clothes. As I settled down for what became an hour-long wait, I tried small talk with my neighbours.

On my left sat a tall, glamorous, familiar-looking woman not much older than myself, who seemed to know everybody in the room. Except me, but that didn't stop her from asking who I was and writing her name and number for me in my open and ready notebook. She was an enterprising former pop singer from a girl-band who had married into a wealthy industrialist family in the city. On my right sat... I had no idea. Efforts at making eye contact bore no fruit and I was, for her, invisible.

Now a fashion show, I realized consequently, can be sliced into three unequal pieces.

The first piece is the biggest: waiting. This forms a substantial but not inconsequential part of a fashion show. There is the anticipation, the crowds, the bling, the perfumes, the high level

FIGURE 1: The Main Show Area

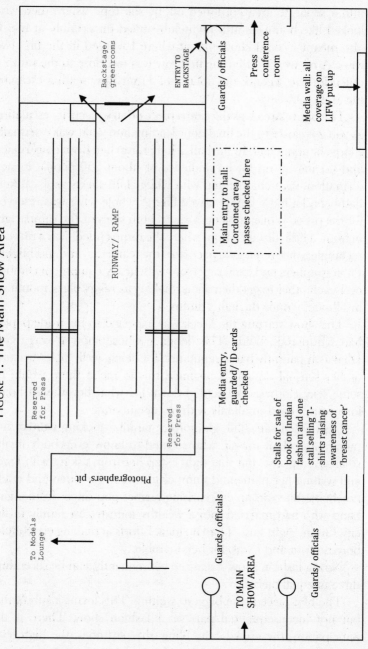

drama around entry, denying people entry, keeping paparazzi in control. Shows often started late, with the waiting period before a show being an opportunity for people in the audience (who usually know one another) to socialize. The cause for the delay was not always clear; on some occasions it appeared to be a wait for a special guest (although there were no official 'chief guests'), on others it appeared to be a technical delay. During this time, people meet and greet. Chit chat. Look through one another. All of these also have an important function: to be seen at Fashion Week and establish oneself as relevant participants in the industry or part of the city's elite with easy access to a high-security event like this.

The next piece is the thinnest. A sliver that is so precious and sheer that it can be rolled by the finest hands into a small but very expensive and unappetizing piece of sushi. This is the main event, the fashion show. Those 15 minutes that wing by too quickly but make up the show are wildly unpredictable.

The third piece is a medium-sized workable retail piece, the one that's value for money, that's about business. It's the after-show when the lights come back on, and media descend on socialites for bytes, the designers accept pats on their backs while watching buyers from the corner of her/his eye to gauge their responses, and models scurry about backstage stumbling out of their show clothes to get ready for the coming show. Next.

As the lights dimmed though, indicating that finally the show was going to begin, I caught the excitement that rippled through the audience like a wave, and a thrill went down my spine. The collection was presented in the ambience of a nightclub, complete with barstools and pole dancing. Models in sequined lycra shimmered as they leaned back, perching on barstools set up on the ramp, or arching against the yellow poles, raising their arms languidly. Some swung around a pole, simulating practised dance moves. One of the taller ones rubbed her lower back on a pole and slid down slowly, awkwardly splaying her long legs like Bambi learning to walk.

I pushed down some anxieties about this being a tad voyeuristic and rather suggestive. These were things we saw everyday around us, on billboards, on TV, in supplements of newspapers. Yet the proximity of the audience to the ramp made the experience intimate and different, especially from as up close and personal as the second row. At times, the proximity could be unnerving as glistening legs, backs and midriffs walked past under blinding spotlights, which showed up every pore on the model's body. Any scars, blemishes, imperfections in make-up, even a twitch in a model's smile were immediately visible under this light.

Also surrendering to the lights were those sitting in the Front Row. This first row of seats nuzzling the ramp, only an arm's length away, was really an extension of it. The audience could see the ramp, but also visible and basking in its reflected light were the occupants of the Front Row. Photos of the runway inevitably catch the Front Row, and those sitting here (and therefore being seen and photographed) are part of the broader performance of the show.

—m—

In 168 hours, to my dissatisfaction, my 'field' had been wrapped up. I had to wait for it to reconstitute itself when I returned the next year for a second attempt at being an 'insider'. The organizers had given in to my persistent follow up and provided me a few show passes and seminar passes. LIFW 2005 continued to be held at the Grand Hyatt hotel but now had a more business-like feel.

The space was more organized, with a new temporary exhibition space constructed for designers and the main sponsor Lakmé offering a space for 'image consultancy', trials of their products, and opportunities to be 'made over' by expert hairdressers and make-up artists. Other sponsors also had lounges and stalls to showcase their wares. Media rooms fitted with computers and internet access were available. The paranoia about access remained. Uniformed guards as well as staff were omnipresent, diligently marking out which spaces were accessible to public or off bounds, glaring at diffident youngsters or outright asking those who seemed a bit lost what business they had there.

The exhibition space for designers' stalls was a makeshift white tent, still under construction even after the week had begun. Each stall was done up in the designer's signature aesthetics. I crossed a popular punk designer's stall done up with pink fur and leather couches, while another designer known for opulent traditional wear had brocade drapes on the wall. The tent was inefficiently air-conditioned with open shafts visible at various places in the roof. As I crossed stalls being set up, one designer worried aloud that it looked like it might rain. As the stalls did not have lockable doors, another designer was concerned that the expensive garments could be stolen or damaged overnight. Transporting all the pieces to and fro was not feasible and could damage the garments. Having their own caretaker stay the night on the premises to guard a stall was not acceptable. By the next morning a solution has been found: sliding canvas shutter doors had been constructed overnight and entry had been cordoned off for those without a delegate pass.

Sitting through some fashion shows through the day (always in sorry corner seats, far from the hallowed second row of the previous year), it seemed designers were trying to put forth a more professional face. On each seat was a press kit comprising one or two photographs of a model displaying some select creation, a press note or abstract poetic rabble about the inspiration behind the collection and contact details for the designer. More enterprising designers would have a 'cue sheet' to detail each item being exhibited with a reference number, technical details and the name of the model wearing the item so that the audience could follow it on the ramp (often, this was incorrect).

In some shows you could be excused for wondering about what was so conceptual about being 'inspired by Morocco', as one show noted in their press note. Some designers' wares seemed straight off the streets of Bangkok. But some showcased interesting innovations and techniques that, for an outsider like me, did indeed seem novel. Like an origami inspired dress, or a technique that seamlessly melded silver foil or warq on textiles just like on a diamond shaped kaju barfi.

Designers appeared to be struggling, though, to find what could be Indian yet international. What could be the meeting point between Indian sensibilities, the cornerstones of which are over-the-top embellishments and loud bridal trousseaus, and the international market: a worshipper of silhouettes and monotones? How could they reconcile the absence of four traditional seasons in India and the strictly seasonal fashion calendar of the international market? This remained the central conflict in designs that appeared over and over again these two years at LIFW.

Like someone drawing, wiping clean and redrawing on a whiteboard in a loop, trying to arrive at that perfect confluence of India-meets-the-world and establish a distinct identity as a designer with unique sensibilities, that would transform the little ramp in the banquet hall into the tarmac runway of the airport from which they could launch their international careers.

—⁕—

'The Fashion Week is to us what the budget is to the *Economic Times*', said Nonita Kalra, then editor of *ELLE* India, as we settled down in the lobby bar for an interview. She was echoing what she had said that morning at the Business of Fashion seminars, where I had approached her. We sat in the Foster's Lounge area in the lobby, an informal social space set up by one of the sponsors (Foster's) where one could have a beer and watch an ongoing show being projected on a large screen or a photo-shoot happening in another corner. As we sipped our 4 pm vodkas at 250 rupees a drink, she talked about the history of the magazine, and where Indian fashion was at.

'We as a society have always been fashionable,' she insisted. 'Think of the sari, the shringar, even my bai likes to have fresh flowers in her hair every morning. Glamour has always been important to us, look how we worship our heroes in Bollywood. It's nothing new to us, just the internationalization that's happening now.' Which is what her magazine capitalizes on. The magazine is aimed at 18 to 35 year olds, young urban women, 'women like you' she waved at me.

'I don't know about the girl in the village. I can't talk to her. I'd have to learn the ethos and work in an NGO,' she smiled. But girls in Delhi and Bombay, where circulation for the magazine is highest, 'every girl wakes up and combs her hair and worries about her fat arse', and that's where her magazine fits right in.

What about cosmetic surgery, I asked? 'I'm personally very anti cosmetic surgery', she said, 'but the magazine won't say anything about it. We maintain a strategic silence'. We turned to chatting about LIFW. Why Lakmé, though, I asked? Nowhere else in the world does the fashion week belong in name to a company.

'But who else will do it?'

Two perfumed ladies stopped by to greet the petite editor with air kisses. One was 'dying for a cigarette' and bummed one off me, the other 'dying for a drink' drank out of Nonita's glass. She introduced me vaguely, not forgetting to mention that we had both gone to the same school (found out in the course of the interview) which brought forth a smile from the ladies. 'This one's a beautiful, strong girl' said the one in the black off-shoulder top to me, putting her arm around Nonita. The one with the streaked hair was furtively smoking, 'don't want the cameras to catch me like this' she winked.

A bell rang to announce the next show in 10 minutes, by designer Malini Ramani, to which they had passes and I didn't. The trio said their goodbyes and moved towards the silken rope, while I sat back to finish my drink and watch the show being flashed live on the screen in the lounge.

Ramani's show was called 'Carnival Chic' about 'three girls celebrating life', the voiceover said. The show of clothes was woven around three characters and the transformation they go through. First up was Maya who was bored, bored, bored; a material girl whose primary activity was shopping before she 'finds herself'. Then there was Maria, a schoolgirl 'tormented by temptations' who goes to church one fateful Sunday and transforms. Shedding her all-girls school uniform she discovers lust, desire and runs riot with colour, all glowing eyes and swaying hips. 'Sex, magic, makeover' said the husky voiceover. The last caricature was of Tara, older, divorced and wondering about the futility of life. Ashram-like clothes appear, she is puzzled, she is searching and finally in a mystical swirl she discovers her true dream (which, it turns out, was to be a fashion designer). As the characters transform to find inner peace, temple bells sound and the show climaxes in a haze of saffrons, oranges and marigolds with a Bharatnatyam pose thrown in for good measure.

I guessed Ramani's target audience to be largely foreign tourists in Goa. Her collection had also found a keen audience in the group of young men sitting at the table next to mine, especially the raunchy set of carnivalesque clothes in the middle segment through which they had chuckled and pointed out models to one other, and passed lewd comments around with a bowl of peanuts. These men didn't seem to be participants in LIFW in any way, just regular Delhi lads with the money and status to walk into a five star hotel and sit around for an evening drink. Today, by design, they had some entertainment on the side.

Outside the low 'wall' that enclosed the Foster's Lounge, the lobby buzzed with activity. The lobby was a microcosm in itself of swarming creatures, a confluence, where streams of different types of people converged. Retail specialists, handloom experts, trend forecasters, fashion journalists, public relations professionals, buyers from international and regional chains, teachers and students from fashion design institutes, and a large contingent of aspiring models – more male than female, not participating in the Fashion Week but taking their chances at being discovered by a discerning and famous eye.

Standing in the lobby, I was reminded of labour 'chowks' in Jaipur: a road crossing where daily wage labourers stand early every morning to be picked by contractors, mainly for construction work. The lobby was a chowk of a different kind. These 'models' (some never actually having modelled before) came diligently every morning and sat cooling their heels till the evening, unable to access most of the event, not even going in to the Foster's Lounge to have a drink as it would cost them, but knowing that somehow they had to be there. Some enterprising ones would approach influential people passing by, introduce themselves and exchange telephone numbers, soliciting work. I turned to escape a male aspiring model who, despite my protestations, had been pursuing me to help him get work.

Round the corner shimmered a polyester mass of giggling girls eating aloo bondas, slurping Coke and chatting loudly in Punjabi. It was a tour group of 15 young women from Hoshiarpur, Ludhiana, Phagwada and Chandigarh led by a male supervisor.

FIGURE 2: The Lobby Area

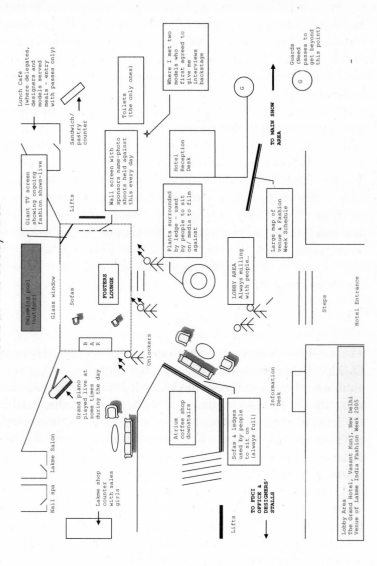

Lunch Café
(where delegates,
designers and
models served
meals – entry
with passes only)

Sandwich/
pastry
counter

Giant TV screen
showing ongoing
fashion shows–live

Toilets
(the only ones)

Where I met two
models who
first agreed to
give interviews
backstage

Wall screen with
sponsors name–photo
shoots held against
this every day

Hotel
Reception
Desk

Lifts

Swimming pool
(outdoor)

Glass window

Sofas

POSTERS
LOUNGE

Plants surrounded
by ledge – used
by people to sit
on/ media to film
against

Large map of
venue & Fashion
Week Schedule

TO MAIN SHOW
AREA

Guards
(Need
passes to
get beyond
this point)

G

G

B
A
R

Onlookers

LOBBY AREA
Always milling
with people...

Steps

Hotel Entrance

Grand piano
played live at
some times
during the day

Atrium
coffee shop
downstairs

Sofas & ledges
used by people
to sit on
(always full)

Information
Desk

Nail spa   Lakme Salon

Lakme shop
counter with sales
girls

Lifts

TO FDCI
OFFICE &
DESIGNERS'
STALLS

Lobby Area
The Grand Hotel, Vasant Kunj, New Delhi
Venue of Lakme India Fashion Week 2005

They were Lakmé's 'best salesgirls' who had been selected from different districts and awarded with a 'prestigious exposure trip' to LIFW in a Lakmé sponsored bus that had come in the morning and was to take them back later that day. 'So what did you think?' I asked the cheery, excited, delighted group. They enjoyed it a lot, they had a blast, their parents and husbands were very proud, they have done beauty courses, they love lip-liners, come a gaggle of responses.

I strayed a little further and sat on some steps to write notes. Two model-like apparitions sat a few steps away, also eating aloo bondas. By now I was wondering where they were getting the aloo bonda from because I could really have done with one myself. The two ladies were models, they admitted when I asked, but as their accent verified, they were models from the UK and just here to 'check out an Indian fashion week'. 'Sorry, can't really say we'd 'ave much te say te you,' said the blonde one. Frustrated at not having found my key into the real action yet, I traipsed back to the lobby in search of the toilets. And then suddenly, unannounced, my fortune turned.

—⁓—

The day I met Vinita was perhaps the most significant day in my PhD life. If I hadn't bumped into her and another model, Bianca, outside the hotel toilets near the lobby; if I hadn't exclaimed and said, 'Please. I need your help'; if she hadn't smiled warmly at my nervous request and said in her strange accent 'Come and meet me backstage tomorrow. We'll talk between hairstyling and make up', things would have been very different. 'My sisters are academics, PhDs' she told me later. 'I understand.'

Entry backstage was off limits even for those with passes. My 'meeting her backstage' therefore wasn't going to be a cakewalk. I feebly argued with the fierce gatekeeper appointed there that I wasn't a random crasher. The guard looked at me like he'd heard people say this every day but could I show him a pass? I called out to a girl with a walkie-talkie passing by inside and asked her to request Bianca or Vinita to come to the entry. Bianca came chewing gum and fiddling with a curly strand of hair, my future in her hands. 'Umm. Oh. Sorry. Not now but... I'll check if Vinita will see you.' But this exchange in English was enough for the guard to know I wasn't bluffing and he grudgingly let me through.

I was in.

'Backstage' was a big tent attached to the show area with three makeshift greenrooms, two for female and one for male models. Each greenroom was an air-conditioned tent with white canvas 'walls' and uneven grey carpets. The rooms were flooded with white light.

Trolleys of clothes rolled in an out, and acted as movable walls, neatly splitting the room into cubicles. Each 'cubicle' had a long table set against the wall, a waist-length mirror about 2 metres wide, with plastic garden chairs. This space was shared by two models along with their 'helpers' – students of fashion design, on duty to help models get in and out of clothes.

'How many models are there in each room?' I asked Vinita's helper as I waited at her cubicle. 'Count the mirrors and multiply by two,' she said. According to my calculations then, there were 16 models in each greenroom. Two groups of models were doing shows alternately, with a total of about 40 shows scheduled through the week.

'There's just too much in Fashion Week,' Vinita yawned apologetically as we began. 'Fittings for 19 designers, you wake up at 8 am, finish at 9 pm, and all you want to do is splank yourself on the bed and go to sleep.' Vinita was just starting to get ready for the next show. She was warm and chatty but warned: 'Whatever you ask, I'll tell you, but don't ask my age. That I can't tell you.'

Vinita was a Person of Indian Origin whose forefathers had migrated to a small island country in the Caribbean some generations ago. Coming from an orthodox Maharashtrian family ('a family of academics'), she had moved ('moved back I suppose no?' she mused) to Bombay at the age of 16 (I tried to stop myself from doing the math and arriving at her age) in the mid 1990s after being discovered by a well known fashion photographer and winning a local beauty contest. She worked in Bombay for four years but it was a nightmare.

'First time, Bombay came as a shock to me. Traffic, noise, being alone, no family… I was too young. I missed home too much and soon packed my bags and went back.' But the offers kept coming, and Vinita returned to do some ad campaigns that went on to become a spectacular success.

Halfway through her life story, the helper of one of the fashion designers showing later in the week created a minor distraction by calling for everyone's attention. Dumping a pile of strange looking footwear with tentacle-like extensions in the middle of the room, she announced that all models' helpers come forth to take the designated shoes for a trial. Vinita's pair didn't fit. 'My size is 8 and 5, length of 8 and fit of 5,' she explained to the confused helper patting her hands comfortingly, but handing the shoes back. She added a special request, 'And PLEASE give me flats!'

The next distraction came when we moved down the assembly line to the hairstyling desk. The models' hair for this particular show was being put up into tight Miss India style buns on which tiaras could be comfortably placed. The process seemed heavy on the blow dry and involved a considerable amount of pulling back every strand of hair. Vinita winced and 'ouch'ed through a trying 15 minutes, finally snapping at the hairdressing guy in Hindi. 'What are you doing? You'll pull it off! Itna kheench kyon rahe ho?' From here she (and I, in tow) moved to final make up, before returning to the hairstyling section. At the end of the assembly line was the star hairdresser waiting to put the finishing touch – a bejeweled headpiece, a band of crusty gems to be placed across the forehead.

Vinita let out a delighted gasp and stroked the headband in wonder. 'It's BEAUTIFUL no?' 'Can I keep it,' she asked JJ, the designer whose show it was, twice. Either JJ didn't hear her or didn't want to, because no reply was forthcoming. It was almost show time and our interview was more or less over.

'I like you,' she said disarmingly as we parted ways. 'You're easy to talk to. Let's keep in touch.' The room began to fill up as models streamed in for their headpieces from a now invisible but audible JJ, who was two heads shorter than all the models.

Through the glitter of shining gems she called out and waved as I moved back to let the tide in. 'Good luck.'

—〰—

That week, I stayed backstage, emerging only to make the long trek to the toilets and keeping the guard informed of my bowel movements. I felt like Alice down the rabbit hole as half-dressed women floated around me, now-in-chiffon, now-in-lycra, with their hairdos changing every two hours. Fastidious organizers and bossy choreographers shouted orders and called out lists six times a day. Designers occasionally hyperventilated. If people wondered who I was, they didn't ask. The diversity backstage (helpers, make up and hair teams, organizers) was wide enough to accommodate a little lady with a notebook.

The helpers were mostly young girls from National Institute of Fashion Design, the premier fashion design college. Being a helper was a form of work experience for these fashion design students. Though peripheral while the model was present, they were the silent hands that kept everything going.

Helpers of designers would instruct them on how to wear a certain garment, footwear or accessory, or put together the required 'look'. This was not altogether an easy task; the footwear in some shows was particularly strange and difficult to manage. The helpers were not known by their own names, but with reference to the model they were aiding as 'Lakshmi's helper' or 'Jesse's helper'. The designers' helpers would call out these 'names' to hand over items to the helper, and the models' helpers would respond accordingly. Managing everything on the trolley and getting the model changed from one outfit to another in the given time was the responsibility of the helper. Other than this, they did not socialize or converse with the models.

Soon, I learnt the protocol of privacy in a public space like a common greenroom. Avoiding eye contact while the model tried on things, staying out when both models were in their cubicle or not going into the greenroom immediately after a show as the models would be changing. I attuned myself to the rhythms of backstage: to tell how far we were from the next show (were the models still at base or had they gotten through hair and moved onto lipstick?), when a show was about to end (was the star model in the star outfit making her way to the wings?), when there would be ennui filled hours to kill such that models would be happy to sit and chat with me, when to stay away from the military drill-like moments of beady eyed choreographers, and when famous designers or celebrities could be expected (because, champagne).

Before a show there would be much excitement and stress. The models, all dressed up, came out of the greenrooms and stood closer to the area between the greenroom and the ramp.

The path from the greenroom to the ramp and back was narrow and crowded with sundry persons – helpers of designers, make up and hair persons for last minute touch ups – becoming a dense space during shows. As each model hurried clumsily through this space, she would transform herself into the very example of lazy poise and confident self-control once in the spotlight. On exiting the ramp, once again her demeanour changed as she hurried back through the same path (squeezing past another model hurrying in the opposite direction for her entry) with skirt lifted to change into the next outfit allotted to her. Following a quick change, she would return for a repeat.

In one show that required a particularly fragile hairstyle, a hair stylist with a hairspray was positioned at the point between the ramp and greenroom and as each model went onto the ramp she would lower her head like a Japanese greeting towards the hairspray man, and he would spray it onto her hairdo. And so on for each model. When each came back after walking the ramp, another spray would be showered on them to ensure that the hairdo did not disintegrate while they changed. Once they were back after the change, it was time for yet another round of spray before they got onto the ramp again. Soon the area reeked of hairspray, and everyone went home nauseous, having inhaled copious amounts of chlorofluorocarbons.

After the show, the press would sometimes make their way into the greenroom to take bytes from models or designers.

FIGURE 3: A Bird's Eye View of Backstage

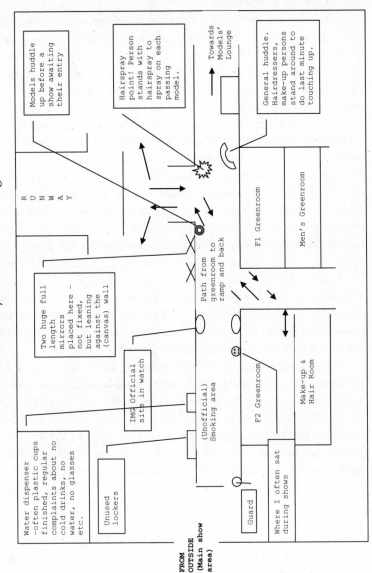

Occasionally, one could hear the post-show press conference being held in the adjoining room.

One morning, suddenly, a press conference was held out of turn. Loud voices and excited babble indicated many more attendants than usual. A controversy had erupted. The director of FDCI spoke first, hinting at the seriousness of matters. A male voice followed. It was designer Suneet Varma, accusing a fellow designer Aki Narula of having copied one of Varma's designs for the Bollywood film 'Bunty aur Babli'. Varma had come across a photo of actress Rani Mukherjee in the outfit in pre-release publicity stills for the film, and been shocked to find it was one of his creations ('it's a complete rip-off from my Fall/Winter 2003 collection', he stated) being passed off as someone else's. 'It's shameless. I plan to take action against the movie, its producers, the designer concerned and the actress.' The 'designer concerned' was Aki Narula, responsible for doing costumes for the film.

By afternoon this was all everyone could talk about. Then suddenly, another unscheduled press conference. This time, it had been called by Aki Narula clarifying matters, saying the controversial piece of clothing had merely been sourced by his teams from a shop in Mumbai without any label and used for the film shoot with no knowledge of it being a Varma rip-off.

Now so far, things had been running like clockwork. Like anywhere else, there had been the odd skirmish, a few glitches with a fair amount of healthy gossip thrown in. But this was different. For the first time, cracks in the surface began to show and like an onion the layers began to peel off. The Alice in Wonderland feeling was waning and as the first skin was shed, with no-more-stars-in-my-eyes I watched the hierarchies and the politics unravel.

—m—

One afternoon, some of the older models walked by towards the make-up room with glasses of white wine in their hands. One came back to give a flute of champagne to a supermodel who was putting in a special appearance that day. The newer generation of models watched enviously, as did the helpers. Wine and champagne weren't a regular feature, but it was part of the 'style' of some of the more flamboyant designers to have this extra for the models. Not for all the models though.

Unspoken rules governed who partook in the wine drinking and who didn't. Who received the designers' grandest outfit and who received the skimpiest. Whose request for a change in outfit was entertained and who had no say in the matter. Who communicated as an equal with the designer/choreographer/star hairdresser and who, like a new bride, maintained a respectful silence in the presence of 'elders'.

A division existed between older and younger generations of models. An unwritten code of conduct demanded that correct posturing of 'senior-junior' relations be always maintained. Older and more established models (some were new but had made it big quickly) commanded more respect, a greater price in terms of the money they charged, and exercised more power. They were often given the privilege of starting or ending a show, or walking the ramp with the designer at the end. Models with some film connection (even a small bit role in a marginal film) were often given star treatment, bringing out the hallowed position that Bollywood enjoys in the glamour industry. Others with some class privilege – being an NRI or from a wealthy background or just having an accent – were able to, in some cases, move between ranks or transcend the boundaries marked out for newcomers. The models with perceptibly shaky English and small town antecedents remained mostly on mute.

Designers often gave 'more special' outfits to the established models, as they would expect the audience to recall them more easily, or the press to photograph them. Some designers paid special attention to established models and personally touched up their look before they went on the ramp. Some seniors had an obvious rapport and familiarity with the designers and choreographers ('we're old friends'; 'we started our careers together'; 'he made my Miss India clothes'), whereas newer models were to be seen and not heard.

All shows were also not equal. A famous designer's show had an added appeal for the models, as did shows where the designer was a friend, or the clothes themselves were different and costume-like, making the models feel they were part of a creative enterprise. Designer Sabyasachi's show was one such, where the energy was contagious as he jumped up and down with a dizzy excitement and the models looked in wonder at their own transformation into an unglamorous avatar, wearing spectacles and in a librarian's bun with books as accessories, in a collection (later considered path-breaking and bought out by Selfridges) mysteriously titled 'The Nair Sisters'.

Choreographers and designers, and some famous make-up artists, wielded considerable influence, and models often walked on eggshells when interacting with them. One morning, a well-known make-up artist admonished one of the newer models who had asked her to apply her base foundation, a menial job. 'Get one of my assistants to do that!' she snapped. Her relationship with the established models was more equitable and friendly. Established models were able to confront make-up artists more easily— one prominent model for instance made no bones about how they were not taking off the make-up properly after a show and were responsible for some rashes. Another spontaneously took an assistant hairdresser to task for burning some hair while crimping the hair for a certain hairstyle.

Another afternoon, when the supermodel Niharika was being personally attended to by designer duo Abu and Sandeep and their helpers and being draped in white, a senior model Bianca passed by eating something. It was not her show and she was just hanging around in her everyday clothes. She tried to feed a bit to Niharika who complied. One of the designer duo jokingly boomed in a loud voice, 'NO EATING WHILE DRESSING UP!', trying to make light of what for him was possibly a serious issue of law and order (their collection after all was all-white) and perhaps trying to be loud enough to ensure that others heard it and read it as a rule to be followed. Bianca too made light of the admonishment and shot back saying, 'It could be taken as sabotage, no?'

Although mentioned in jest, the word 'sabotage' brought to light the fragile space that it is backstage when people who may otherwise be competitors, share it.

Bianca as an established model could behave in a certain way and basically get away with it. This was also because the person she was feeding and who was complicit in the act was also an established model who was doing a special favour to the designers by appearing in their show! The scene would have turned out differently if newer or lesser-known models were involved.

The juniors stepped back when it came to the use of the full-length mirrors in between the greenroom area and the ramp. Just before the show was to start, many models would practise their 'look' or an expression or just pose and admire themselves in front of these two full-length mirrors. While all of them caught a fleeting glimpse of themselves before proceeding to the ramp, a few would stand longer in front of the mirror. Newer models rarely took this liberty.

In the case of male models this was not so: all of them seemed to want to see themselves in the full-length mirror. The maximum number of trips to these mirrors, and maximum time in front was shared by male models – particularly one popular male model, who even when not dressed for a show and was just passing by would stand arrested by his own image in the mirror and pose, checking his profile.

Amongst the women, one particular supermodel spent a long time looking at herself in the full length mirrors cocking her head from side to side. No one could ask her to move and allow space for others to use the mirrors as she was evidently amongst the biggest names there.

After the politics of seniority, patronage, class and association, there was also the politics of gender. On the last day, I entered the backstage area and was surprised to find it deserted. A few helpers hung around chatting on table-tops, one or two models sat texting on their mobiles, or with their heads down on their tables to take a quick nap. The lull was because the next show was a 'men only' show. It's well known that the modelling world has a predominance of women, and that fashion has historically catered to dressing women. Indeed, male models had much less work most of the days. They would often be just hanging about, scheduled to show just two outfits in the entire day, perhaps only for one show. Female models did get more attention, but this did not seem to deter the large number of male models milling around. The previous year, some prominent male models had staged a walkout, alleging that they were being discriminated against. These feelings lingered in the air even as the number of male models seemed to have increased from one year to the next.

—⁂—

Fashion weeks are the annual festival of the fashion community, where the industry's members come together in a bounded space for a limited time; an occasion where they draw the boundaries of who matters and who doesn't. It is a social ceremony, usually closed to outsiders. It's an exclusive event for a certain set of people held in an exclusive venue with boundaries that separate the well heeled from the flat, the insiders from the outsiders.

In 2006, FDCI announced that there would be two fashion weeks every year instead of one, so that designs for different seasons could be exhibited as in the rest of the world. This way, Indian fashion could be integrated into the international market so that a greater volume of business could be done. After this announcement came another – the split between the Lakmé and FDCI, the end of a six-year partnership. Lakmé (and event organizer IMG) announced that it would have its own fashion week in Mumbai, while FDCI would have another – the original and official India Fashion Week – in Delhi. Wills Lifestyle, the apparel retail wing of a tobacco conglomerate, came forth to sponsor the FDCI fashion week, which then came to be known as the Wills Lifestyle India Fashion Week (WLIFW), pointing to the rising clout of the retail industry which had been the fastest growing sector that year.[20] (Consequently, Amazon India became the main sponsor in 2014, reflecting the phenomenal rise of online retail.)

The scale and form of Fashion Week changed once again in 2007 when the venue of what was now WLIFW was moved out of a five star hotel to the trade fair halls at Pragati Maidan in Delhi – the very spot where fashion shows in India had begun their journey in the early 1980s as part of textile trade exhibitions. Visitors to this Fashion Week were agreed that at this large, industrial venue, the India Fashion Week was now more similar to its international counterparts and heralded its transformation to a truly 'trade and business' event.

In other parts of the world, meanwhile, fashion weeks were actually going out of fashion. An article in the *Guardian* screamed 'The catwalk, darling? It's so last year.'[21] Most orders for new designs were previewed and placed much before fashion week. In India, a retail specialist pointed out at a conference that 'a ramp show is important in making a new relationship. But not important in the long run.' A fashion show may help a designer establish his aesthetics, but it is, in fact, not so central to the business of fashion.

This is ironic considering the media circus and security around the sacred main show area, and the baited breath with which an audience sits to watch the lights come on, the music begin and the dazzling parade of a dozen young women walking down the ramp. While the spectacle keeps the audience rooted to their seats, the real business continues elsewhere.

WORK

Six o clock already/ I was just in the middle of a dream
I was kissing Valentino by a crystal blue Italian stream.
But I can't be late/ Coz then I guess I just won't get paid
These are the days when you wish your bed was already
made…

'Manic Monday', Bangles. 1986

You cannot *stuff* yourself with desserts every evening and
be as beautiful as the others who are really working hard
for it.

Vinita, model in her late twenties.

CHAPTER SEVEN

Mannequin

Dear Notebook Nalini*,

My dad doesn't consider my work seriously – he still says, oh you should start working now. And I say, but I AM working! They don't see this as real work.

The day he said this to me, I had just returned from a disastrous shoot for a well-known mobile phone company. The call time was 4 am. I get there and things don't start before 8 am, although I have to start getting ready and everything. It was a really HOT day, and we were shooting continuously. It was a Sunday and so they told us the AC was not on in the building we were in.

By afternoon I was almost passing out, and by 3 pm I just could not perform under the circumstances. Then it got delayed, and they were like 'Just last few shots, then you can go'. Even though I could barely stand, I was trying to keep my cool. I mean from 4 am to 4 pm, it was like being a slave worker. Finally I cracked. I said, please get me a cab RIGHT NOW. I am leaving. Somehow I did the last shots, and waited for the cab.

The cab had no AC in it. I broke down and started crying. Here I was working so hard for them and they were not even considerate enough to get me an AC cab?

I want to say to my father, modelling is a job like any other. How can I make him see that what I do is real work?

Tina from GKII

* My imaginary avatar as agony aunt, but based on actual conversations and narratives of the women interviewed.

Dear Tina from GKII,

Your dad is not the only one. Who thinks of models as labouring bodies, and modelling as 'real work'? 'You wear some nice clothes and sashay down the ramp. That's all,' I heard someone say once. 'Sashay' – a nice word on all counts, but makes it sound like a breeze.

I too was surprised to see that modelling is demanding physical work. All that up and down a ramp in heels. Ad-shoots through 36-hour shifts. The photo-shoots on slippery rocks, in harsh weather, neck deep in cold water, for long stretches of time in odd positions. A beauty queen of the nineties said to me of her first shoot: 'It was December and freezing. My first outfit was a bra top with silver sequins, leggings and accessories like a stole and other heavy jewellery. It was early morning and the shoot was at the fountains at Rashtrapati Bhawan…even in the photos you could see the goose-bumps on my flesh.'

December. Delhi. Early morning.

Would I get out of my Jaipuri quilt before dawn and slip into a bra top to pose atop a fountain at Rashtrapati Bhavan in two degree centigrade? I think not. 'It's hard work in a different way,' she had said to me, 'Sometimes you work from 6 am to 2 am the next morning.'

Noelle, another of your seniors, told me:

'Doing an ad film or music video is very hectic. If the director or agency calls for a rehearsal, that is the worst because they don't mind rehearsing with you from 7:00 in the evening with full make-up on till 3:00 in the morning. You work around the clock until they call it a wrap. No sleep, no going home, nothing. Through all of that everyone else can look tired and be sweaty, and have their hair flying out…but you have to be as fresh as a daisy.'

'There are no working rules in the industry,' Noelle told me, although she learnt to set her own rules: 'At a still shoot I shoot only for eight hours,' she said. 'I cannot possibly look like a model after eight hours. If you shoot 50 pictures in that time, good for you; if you shoot only two, too bad.'

Tina, maybe you could try to list down the kinds of tasks you do. Walk him through your work day. Speak to your father. Let him into your work life. If that doesn't work, take solace in the fact that most of what most women do (through the day, through the week, through the year) is unrecognized labour and either unpaid or underpaid.

—⁓—

Dear Notebook Nalini,

A strange thing happened the other day. I went for an ad-film shoot, reaching before sunrise for my make up and hair. It was like five in the morning. The director's wife – who is an industry veteran herself – said to me, 'My God! How can you come with no make-up on? Look at yourself! You don't look like a model.'

I was alarmed.

I told her, 'Ma'am, I sent you my portfolio and a video recording of my work. That is what I look like when I am at work. This is what I look like normally.' Having been part of the industry for so long, surely she should know better?

Noelle from Gurgaon

Dear Noelle from Gurgaon,

I think it was your junior, Pragati, who said of her first few months in modelling, 'All this time I was looking at people, seeing how they walked, talked, stood, sat…everything. By doing this I learnt a lot, how you should act and carry yourself.'

I remember wondering – how does 'talking, standing and sitting' have anything to do modelling?

Then Gurpreet, five years into the job, broke it down for me: 'I have an image to live up to – of looking glamorous or whatever. The choreographer will sell that *image* to the client, so if I go to the meeting with the client dressed normally, it will fall short of their expectations. The clients are after all *lalas* (shopkeepers). *They* don't know that in front of the camera, or with make-up, you will look like that in the photograph – even if you look ordinary in front of them. They want to see in front of them what will come out in the photo! Otherwise they will say, 'oh yeh ladki? (sniffing nose in disgust) Yeh ladki kya kar degi? (What can this girl do?)'

'Being a model' is a symbol, a euphemism for many things: for being fair, tall, 'classed up', made up and desirable. It involves imbibing a certain way of walking, speaking, looking and behaving as per the rules of the game in your field. There is so much pressure amongst your juniors to continue 'being models' once the spotlight is off.

Even for international stars. British supermodel Naomi Campbell was once quoted as saying, 'If you expect me to be in the kitchen cooking breakfast in high heels, looking as though I just stepped out of a fashion magazine, it's not going to happen.'

Keep resisting. Some day, people outside the industry and those within it will understand that this is your job and you have a life outside it.

—⁊⁊⁊—

Dear Notebook Nalini,

We met at Fashion Week. I was in the lobby and I met you after you were speaking to some of the magazine ladies. I want to be a model but someone told me it is a 'high maintenance job'. Can you help?

Natasha from Navi Mumbai

Dear Natasha from Navi Mumbai,

I was just doing research at Fashion Week. But if it's any help, I'm tearing out a page of my field notebook to share with you the list that I made at Heerina's house. She started modelling recently and drew up this list of 'investments' she's made in the last year to keep herself in the race.

1.   Good clothes to go for auditions and things. You can't walk around just like that in anything.

2.   Bras and underwear – different types (gel bra, strapless, backless, midriff) and colours (black, white, beige, thongs of different colours) – because you need to wear different kinds under different types of garments. Thongs with thin side straps make you look slimmer, whereas ones with fat sides make you look fatter.

3.   Shoes! I have 36 pairs of shoes. Boots, stilettos, sandals, ethnic, in different colours – black, white, beige, gold, silver.

Because these go with most things. These are expensive. So when a pair is flicked from the greenroom it hurts! Nowadays clients want you to bring your own shoes.

4. Accessories – Jewellery, watches, scarves, belts, bags.

5. Portfolio, costs between 15-20,000 rupees. Usually includes the 5,000 rupees given to the make-up man.

6. Best products for your skin, make-up that you want to use, if you don't want to use cheap make-up which is sometimes provided by the organizers. Sometimes the client will give you 1,000 rupees extra for doing your own make-up.

7. Hair straightener – lots of models carry that.

8. Petrol costs as you have to go to many auditions and meet people.

9. A comp card (a compact card which shows some of your portfolio). Each such card costs 100 rupees.

10. Folio pictures are also expensive to keep getting done but you need to have them.

11. Contact lenses, lots of models keep them. I feel uncomfortable with contact lenses so I don't wear them. But others keep all shades – cat-eyes, sea green, grey, blue, hazel.

12. False eyelashes (stuck on with eyelash glue). For every show we use false eyelashes.

13. Other odd items from tips you pick up – like there are eye-drops that lot of models use to wash out redness.

14. The gym. That costs 30,000 rupees a year.

Good luck.

—∞—

Dear Notebook Nalini,

My agency has increased my rate from 4,000 rupees to 8,000 rupees per ramp show this season after I was selected for Fashion Week. I should be happy. But I accidentally found out that my best friend in the agency – who joined much after I did – had her rate raised from 4,000 rupees to 18,000 rupees per show! I feel terrible. Why has the agency done this? What have I done wrong to get a much lower raise than my friend?

Roopali from The Agency

Dear Roopali from The Agency,

Did your friend: Get a magazine cover this year? Endorse a famous brand? Act in a memorable TV commercial? Win a beauty contest? Go abroad and do shows for an Armani or Valentino? Or perhaps she landed an appearance or role in a Bollywood feature film? A film in the South, then?

If she did, it would explain why she sped up the rate ladder faster than you. Rate-setting of models is an interesting game. The director of an international agency told me in an interview, 'We see from how much work they are doing, the quality of work they are getting, their demand in the market, and *what we can get away with*.' Emphasis added, of course. Don't take it personally. This ladder is special to your field. Identify what its rungs are and be strategic.

—m—

Dear Notebook Nalini,

I read a phrase the other day: 'Equal pay for equal work'.

In my work we do equal work – wear garments and exhibit them on the ramp – but I don't think the pay is equal. I overheard someone at Fashion Week recently say that some people are paid 3,000 rupees for a show, and others 35,000 rupees for the same show. A film actor who was called in to walk the ramp – that too, only once and not three changes like the rest of us, and the buzz is she was paid a lakh and a half. Can you explain this crazy disparity?

Gurpreet from West Delhi

Dear Gurpreet from West Delhi,

I turn to the words of one veteran supermodel colleague of yours, who said to me: 'An M.F. Husain charges several crores for his painting but a (lesser known artist) Bikash Bhattacharya can't charge that much.'

I think what she meant is: in art or performance, 'equal work' is a slippery concept.

This disparity could be because of the different value society attaches to something (Bollywood is more valued in the current form of society, and so unfortunately any representative of

Bollywood gets more money than 'just a model'). Or it could be attributed to the famous 'x-factor', an intrinsic and intangible element that a certain personality adds just by – being themselves. That adds to the sale-ability of the garments or the image of the designer, or to the quality of the show – just by their presence.

—⁓—

Dear Notebook Nalini,

I have a confession to make. I try not to show it but I was surprised at first when I saw so many of the girls smoking and drinking. Then people talk about how this industry has so much sex, drugs, and alcohol. And 'sexploitation'. I feel uncomfortable sometimes when I am in the greenroom with other models. Is the industry really so immoral? Should I be worried?

Shivani from Benaras

Dear Shivani from Benaras,

When I read your letter about so many girls smoking and drinking, I thought 'You should come to my college!'

In my interviews, I did hear of one case of addiction, a rising model becoming a 'coke-head' and spiralling out of control, crashing out of the modelling scene – and it was only this one case that would resurface again and again. People loved to talk about it.

But there was no evidence to suggest that women models were smoking or drinking any more or any less than women NGO workers (where I had worked, for example) or women media professionals or women students in colleges in Delhi.

As for 'sexploitation' (a word coined by our clever media), I wonder if you know that your peers do many things to protect themselves from sleazy deals or dangerous situations and sexual harassment. (Like every other girl in Delhi, India and the world I assume.) Many take a friend along for auditions in strange places or with unknown unreferenced clients, some keep pins or pepper sprays in handbags. Some make a point of making their own drinks at parties and not leaving them unattended. Some keep important phone numbers on easy dial. And some complain to the agency or organizers in case of misconduct, occasionally creating a scene and embarrassing the offender in public.

The only kind of 'exploitation' I heard about repeatedly was financial – being underpaid or unpaid for work done, and having no negotiating power to push back and demand what they rightfully earned.

—m—

Dear Notebook Nalini,

It seems like most terms and conditions of work and pay here are 'negotiable' and I am tired of negotiating. I hate it when clients use photographs for a time period or geographical location other than what was decided on without paying us additional charges. As for overtime, nobody wants to pay Indian models overtime. They just want us to 'adjust'. These woes are typical to our Indian work culture and attitude of getting as much work for as little as possible. Do people generally like to pay very little or do you think that's an Indian mantra?

Mary from Kerala

Dear Mary from Kerala,

An international agency director I interviewed said, 'See, where we can get them overtime, we do get them overtime. But *there's never been a system of overtime in India.*' Emphasis added. 'When we bring in a foreign model, there is always that concept of overtime. So after an eight hour shift the client agrees to pay overtime. But with an Indian model, if we try and fight too much about overtime...there are so many models, they will just go and get someone else... Our models tend not to demand overtime also because we have a great rapport with our clients, and the girls are often shooting many times with the same clients. So if it just means one more hour or something, you'd rather do that favour than create a scene.'

I have to say, Mary, there may well be some truth in your interpretation.

—m—

Dear Notebook Nalini,

I have long silky hair, or rather had *long silky hair before a series of incidents.*

Last year I did about five hair shows in which the hair was coloured with very harsh pigments so the colour would catch on quickly. After a month the colour started bleeding, and I had to bleach my hair thrice to get that colour off! So you can imagine my hair has gone for a complete...you know...it was a mess! Then for every show they spray your hair, you've got your hair styled into buns or knots...so it really takes a toll. All that tugging and pulling has resulted in severe hair-loss.

I am used to my physical space being invaded by strangers who come too close to me to measure, clothe, do make-up or style my hair. But we do get hurt if our hair is pulled! Don't they realize we are human?

Swati from Lajpat Nagar

Dear Swati from Lajpat Nagar,

I heard about a show in which all the models were given 'massive hairdos with these heavy headpieces'. Apparently, one of the girls fainted in the line-up just before the show because of the hairdo. She had had her make-up and hair done first, and all that waiting with the weight on her head 'had done it for her', as one of your colleagues put it.

One of your peers said to me: 'Sometimes the designer's vision is so dangerous to models. For all the creative vision, it is we who have to do it, who have to fulfil the vision! They don't think of you as a human being really, just as a puppet who they will mould according to their vision. So if their vision is that you will be all golden, then you will have your hands or arms spray painted with some gold spray – who knows what's in that spray! Or they use glue to stick sequins on you or something on your nails. These are parts of your body, your skin, but they don't really care about what they are putting on you as long as their "vision" is realized.'

I don't know, Swati, what it will take for you and your peers to be seen not just as a canvas for designers to work on, but as collaborators in a creative project. It might be worth sharing these thoughts with those you work closely with, or those you feel might understand.

—⁂—

Dear Notebook Nalini,

What does being 'professional' really mean in this industry?

The other day a choreographer of a fashion show told me that I was being unprofessional for making 'unreasonable demands'. Tell me, is asking to be paid on time, requesting for food that is suitable to our diet patterns, setting a limit on working hours or even asking for a lunch break 'unprofessional'? I'm worried that now she will label me as fussy and difficult. This industry works on word of mouth, and it is too risky for me to be labelled like that.

All the rules about being 'professional' are to be followed by a model, but not the choreographer. A model has to be punctual but the choreographer will walk in throughout the day. The choreographer can postpone their shows and can postpone their dates. They will book our time so we can't take any other job that comes our way, and suddenly, two days before the show, they will cancel it without informing. We have lost the work that way and no cancellation fees are given in India. They do that. But if I back out two days before the show then I will be sued. There are so many double standards here. But we have to bear it. We are not the ones who call the shots.

Gurpreet from West Delhi

Dear Gurpreet from West Delhi,

Thank you for writing again. It took me time to answer your question. I thought for a long time about an incident that one of your newer colleagues Mayuri had told me about. While posing for a photo shoot in a white garment Mayuri accidentally cut her finger on the prop. Instead of crying out in pain and fussing over herself, she put the wounded finger dripping blood at a distance from her body away from the garment – and instead checked to see if the garment had been stained or not.

Mayuri was applauded by the designer for being a true professional, and quickly taken out of the precious garment, before she could tend to her wounded finger. If it seemed a bit awry to me, a case of misplaced priorities, Mayuri didn't think so. This, she felt, was what a professional model should do – put the garments or items in her care above her own personal needs.

It also made me think about my own life and many others around me. How we are slaves to our emails, and feel that answering a mail from our boss or client needs to be done even in the middle of dinner or putting our children to bed. How there is little regard for the overtime many of us put in, the meetings held at odd hours that do not always suit us but that we take grudgingly because we want to be lauded for our professionalism. Even when it doesn't suit us, or might even harm us.

A veteran model lamented to me, 'How do you expect a girl who is working from nine in the morning to 10 in the night, or even one in the night to be thin, when you are giving them burgers and pizzas day in and day out? And then when they put on one inch on the side, you are ready to criticize her!'

Another peer of yours recalled how she was made to understand that by posing in a bikini for a shot, she would be behaving like a true 'professional'. If she refused it would reflect on her as a fussy worker and hamper her chances of better work in the future. She felt she had no choice.

'Professionalism' is a double-edged sword. It is desirable because we all want to be valued and respected as 'professionals'. But 'professionalism' has been used to control or manipulate many of these young women into doing things that they are not fully sure of, like wearing bikinis; or subsidizing costs of the client by doing their own make up; quietly falling in line if there are delays without asking to be compensated; being sprayed with cheap gold paint; undertaking dangerous and painful poses or actions without demands for insurance and so on.

This is true for many when I think of the long hours put in by young people wanting to make good of their careers in urban India today, in jobs where work is carried into the night or into weekends, and any resistance to this way of working is termed 'unprofessional'.

Your words resonated with me for a few days after you wrote to me.

'We are not the ones who call the shots.'

—⁓—

Dear Notebook Nalini,

I recently did this print ad for BED, *a lounge bar in Mumbai, and the tag line was 'Would you go to* BED *with me?' Quite smart I thought.*

But I couldn't believe it and was so hurt when my own boyfriend said, 'I don't think it's right for you to do the ad'.

I said, 'Why not? You also work in the film industry.'

And he said, 'I can't see my wife-to-be... my girlfriend do that.'

But, I said, what is wrong in that? You have known it from the beginning right? What has changed now? I'm not going to be in bed with everybody just because it's written over there! This is what I do. I am wearing very respectable clothes, there is no skin showing anywhere, nothing. There is just the line. So you take it the way you want, or don't take it at all. It's up to you. I am comfortable with what I'm doing, and that's it. Period. If you leave it to the whole world to decide for you, the next thing I know I'll be jumping off the building, that's all. Indian men want women who are very subtle, gharelu and... I AM all that! But there's a time for it! I'm also a professional model. I cannot disrespect my work.

Right?

Vinita from Fashion Week

Dear Vinita from Fashion Week,

You reminded me of what one of your seniors, Shirin, said to me. 'It's a peculiar profession. Where else in the world do you get 15 men to watch you when you are changing, or while you are getting in and out of a tub 100 times trying to do some shampoo ad? Or while you are sighing and breathing and your arms and legs are being shown till up here because it's a waxing ad or a cream ad?'

You could be fighting off a migraine, reminding yourself to pick up aloo-pyaaz on your way back home, or just not feeling too sexy after waiting three hours for the photographer to get his lighting right. But when the lights are on, you will have to pout, arch and look suitably aroused while simultaneously keeping track of what's showing where.

I heard several of your colleagues trying to rationalize and confront this duality: the (bad) girl in front of the camera and the (good) girl away from it. Because they know being a 'bad girl' is punished in our society. One of them said to me: 'If the work requires it, it's ok. It's like playacting. But I don't think anybody would make a show of it after the shot is over.'

Because what happens when the shot is over?

The girls go home to parents, neighbours, boyfriends, partners. And face the impact of this playacting as it spills like ink running past the shooting floor and bleeding into their everyday lives.

Another colleague of yours lamented to me: 'Suddenly the model tag comes on you and suddenly, people feel you are easy, cheap. Men can't believe that you actually have some values and principles after being a model.' The 'model tag' as much as it allows easy entry into nightclubs, adds a film of suspicion in the eyes of onlookers. Even 30 years ago, Shirin saw it. 'There are outsiders who say to me that 'modelling mein aap kitne paise banate ho?' They couldn't imagine you could make this kind of money without sleeping around. In their *heads* you were sleeping around.'

This leads to a strained relationship with the world at large, but the deepest cut is when this cataract affects the ones they love. 'Getting married in India when you are a model is a mammoth job,' said Gurpreet to me. 'No man wants to get serious with a model. You leave modelling in case someone does marry you because he or the family will not tolerate it. Or they will keep cribbing till you compromise. Or you go to a firangi (foreigner). They understand better, they don't have a problem if you are posing in a bikini. They don't think you are a flirt because you are modelling.'

So Vinita, you are justified in your indignation, and you're not alone.

—m—

Dear Notebook Nalini,

I got a call from the office of the owner of a famous fashion magazine in Delhi to be on the magazine cover. He wanted to meet me and see my pictures. He called me to Le Meridien. I said ok I will meet you in the hotel lobby. When I reached I called him, but he said he was sitting at the bar and could I come there? I thought, why is he sitting in the bar when I specified I would meet him in the lobby? Still, I went, found him and sat down. He saw my pictures. And kept looking at me. I wasn't very comfortable with the whole idea of people looking at me. Of course I had my make-up on and I was looking…you know, how people think models should look. Then out of the blue, he said, 'So what else can you do for me?'

We were talking about money then. I told him these are my rates and this is what I would charge. 'No, what else can you do for me?' he asked again.

Then I got it. I asked him straight: oh, I said, are you talking about sexual favours? And he said, 'I think you're smart enough.'

That's it. I just got up, gave him one tight slap. I actually slapped him. It was a shock. I was like…you called me here for this? I told him, what do you think of me? I named a relative who is in politics and said, I'm going to tell her, and I'm going to make your life impossible in Delhi. I just left…

Of course I didn't do those things.

But I was physically shaking as I left, and had an accident within 10 minutes while driving my Maruti because my hands were shaking so much. I couldn't believe it could happen to an honest, hardworking girl like me. You know because…there are certain…sometimes you give certain vibes to somebody. There you can get approached by someone. But knowing myself, when I am not giving that vibe, when I don't fall in that category, when you know I am not like that…

I wanted to speak about him to the press, but then I thought there is no point. I just told my friends, be careful of this man. Imagine, for a magazine cover! You can imagine then what Bollywood would be like! If this guy could ask me it must really be happening, no?

Swati from Lajpat Nagar

Dear Swati from Lajpat Nagar,

Where does one start looking for the history of women as pieces of meat?

When did men assume that women anywhere, anyhow, anytime could be theirs? Who first asked a woman for a sexual favour? Why did she agree? Which woman was the first to tell herself that in a patriarchal world like this, there could be no other way to make it?

We will never know. We won't know because women won't tell. It takes courage to speak out about any kind of sexual violation we face. But it's not because women are not courageous that they won't tell. It's because of something else.

It's because we are taught that such offers are made only to *those kinds of women* – and we will do anything to avoid being labelled as one of them. I learnt the hard way that this is a myth. I learnt that it isn't what you wear or what you do that 'invites' sexual harassment, and that we have nothing to feel guilty for, however much patriarchy tries to volley the blame at us. Sexual harassment happens because people get away with it. Men in power, bosses, teachers, colleagues, even friends. And this neatly woven myth serves them well in getting away with it.

In your head, Swati, there had been a separation between you and women who invited trouble, who asked for it. With this incident you realized that there were no such 'categories'. Still the guilt persisted, and you wondered if being 'dressed like a model' could have been the cause? Perhaps it was better to be silent than to be known as one of *those kinds of women*. Because being known as that would bring even more social punishment, and who wants to deal with that?

Sexual harassment at the workplace is in every profession, including yours.

Some of your peers mentioned to me that they had been offered money for 'services' – but also spoke about how similar things happened to their doctor cousin or management trainee friend at their workplaces. 'These things happen in all professions,' they insisted. And all women. One of your colleagues talked about 'make up men who touch you for a bit too long while applying make up, or the masterjees who take your measurement at fittings – they give that "extra touch" sometimes'. Another talked about how when people say 'oh it's a give and take relationship' repeatedly, she says to them: 'What do you mean by "give and take"?' I give you my services to show your clothes, and take money from you for that work. It is work, and *that* is the give and take.'

All of you are angry about it. One of your colleagues has turned down several 'compromise' offers. She is tired of losing out on work because of her stand, but feels that once someone places a condition on you for work, there will always be a condition to be dealt with. 'I feel like killing them when it happens,' she says. 'I remember once there was a shoot, and they offered me two lakhs. I was like, why are you giving me two lakhs? I only charge

6-7,000 rupees for a shoot. No, they said, you can keep 50,000 for the shoot and rest you know, you need to entertain the client. They don't say you have to sleep with him, they say "entertain the client". You need to go for a dinner and things like that. I was really angry… Why don't you send your mother? Or your sister! You can make better money!'

Till the system proves to you that they won't blame you, that action will be taken, that men won't get away with it, the fight will continue. In your small way you did your bit by warning your friends. Another of your peers said to me, 'See. We do think about it. We should say something, we should boycott. What you can do, you can just tell other people, who are a little close to you, "listen, if somebody calls up just be careful".' But I don't know if it's enough.

--~~~--

Dear Notebook Nalini,

Don't get me wrong. I love what I do – the travel, the clothes, the perks of the job. Holidays on outdoor shoots, stays in luxury hotels, invitations to exclusive parties, introductions to rich and powerful people, getting to be in the media, some amount of fame, and easy entry into clubs. Seeing yourself on billboards and magazines. The joy and pride of being a creative person's muse. Of adding value to their creative process and seeing them journey from being a small designer to a global brand.

But…people perceive models to be dumb. They blindly believe that you have no opinion. They blindly believe a whole lot of shit about models. They believe you are wild, that just because we wear skimpy clothes or whatever on stage, they can stand there looking into a greenroom while we undress. They believe we have no privacy. They believe we are some kind of…two-bit tarts.

And it's not very nice. Because at the end of the day, we are someone's sister, daughter and everything else… It's not fun at all. Because I do some things on the ramp as part of my job, other people perceive you as a titillating sex object.

I don't know how others deal with it, but I just kill them if they stand and be nasty with me out there. With a look, or with words. That's about it. Sometimes it really irritates you and sometimes you're just fed up with it, so you're like whatever. You want to believe I'm dumb? Believe it. If that's what makes your world go around, go ahead.

It's saddening, because people close to you, like parents, they see other people looking at you in a manner... and they are like, tomorrow your daughter might be a model as well, and what will you do then?

Mary from Kerala

Dear Mary from Kerala,

You, Mary, were the most visibly 'empowered' of the women I met. Influential, educated, financially successful, owning a range of assets, living on two continents. Living life on your own terms with your live-in boyfriend and two dogs. You were conscious of your rights, vocal in expressing yourself and it would be foolish to even use the word powerless within a mile's radius of you.

Yet, even in your narrative, 'empowerment' trips over the thick rope of hurt that a decade of the stigma has thrown at you. It is this underlying lack of respectability that keeps your 'empowerment' from being complete.

Perhaps your 'problem with no name',[22] is that.

CHAPTER EIGHT

The Union and the Agency

'The idea to start a models' union came about because there are various problems we face,' said Josy, when I finally settled down for an interview with her at her sunny terrace flat in Mumbai's western suburbs. It hadn't been easy. After accosting Josy in the toilet one Fashion Week I had tracked her for almost three years, following up with the tenacity of a Rottweiler and trying to harmonize our being in the same city.

It had also not been easy because this was a period in her life that Josy did not particularly like talking about.

Josy was about 28 when I met her, having worked in the industry for over 10 years, and having enjoyed a successful stint in Europe in international modelling. She had led an initiative called Models United in Mumbai in 2002 because as she says, 'we wanted that clients and choreographers respect our time and our work.'

Why a union though?[23] 'We studied trade unions in school a lot in Kerala. Didn't you?' she asks. 'We read stories of their success and their strength. A union would represent a body of voices talking together, not one against a hostile jungle. It would protect girls with feeble voices. It's about standing together, being a community. When I was growing up, around us there was always the strong presence of unions. The union ensured that everyone had work. So even the weakest were not left without work or food.'

Josy's idealism shone through every time she repeated herself to those around her, and she garnered enough support for it to become a concrete body. 'At that time, I did not really think what

I was getting into… I just felt that things should be fair. And that I was going into a good thing with a lot of conviction.'

Mobilization for the union began. Lawyers were contracted to register the union in the name of 'Models United'. Within a few months, over 100 women joined the initiative, the majority from Mumbai, but many also from Delhi and Bangalore. Around 25 members were more deeply involved. Over lunches at a white-washed restaurant called Olive (the owner had offered the space for the cause) discussions were conducted over what the mandate of the union was to be, what the problems faced by the women were and what were the minimum standards that needed to be met for any assignment. A set of rules was drafted and a list of 'dos and don'ts' was drawn up regarding late payment, bouncing of cheques, cancellation of shows, hours of work and sexual harassment. A press conference was held to publicize the initiative.

Suddenly the language of the press began to focus on models' working conditions rather than their clothes or cleavage. A ripple of hope ran through the modelling community. However, as the rules began to be implemented and demands were made to choreographers and clients that these conditions be met, the repercussions began.

Within no time, the initiative collapsed.

What went wrong? Josy struggles for the right words.

'Well, picture this. If you have one lion roaring away and all the little animals around stand there by him and support him then there is a chance… But if the lion is roaring away on his own, and the little animals all run away and hide, then the elephant can easily come and stamp on him. That's what happened.'

Josy returned money to those who contributed once the initiative failed to take off. She said, 'There were many things that went wrong, a clash of egos among them, and I needed to save my own career at the end of it, so we dropped it. I was very naïve, and did not realize that I would start losing work seriously because of it. At that time I didn't realize I was a threat to so many people. I also didn't understand that it's an industry of friends, not professionals.' The union crumbled under the weight of members' personal relationships with choreographers and designers, who were the ones wielding power and resisting the demands made by the union.

'The effect of trying to start the union continues till today. It still goes on. People remember. There are still many designers and choreographers who I do not work with or who do not work with me because of the past.'

Since the experiment, there has been little mention of organizing. Josy notes, 'I don't know if there is any possibility of a union in the future. People don't mention the union to me... In fact I am talking about it after many years. But I don't think people feel the need for a union anymore. Once it used to be a topic for passionate discussion amongst us but now people don't discuss it anymore.'

This is not to say the industry had become organized and professional, or that models enjoy equitable terms of work. On the contrary, even as talk of a union became unfashionable, small model coordination companies set up office in all corners of the city as young boys and girls flocked to Delhi and Bombay from all parts of the country to get their foot into the industry's golden door. This combination – of seedy modelling agencies promising to fulfil big dreams, and girls and boys eager to show their talent and waiting for their big break – only made the swelling ranks of models more vulnerable and increased the possibilities of exploitation.

So what changed in the last few years? For the new generation, the union was a concept they could not relate to. The concept of 'unity' itself, or a consolidated front from the models was seen with suspicion, with young girls just out of their teens laughing in the face of any possible unity – even superficial – amongst their peers. 'Aren't models supposed to be selfish?' asked a new entrant to the industry having been fed on a diet of stereotypes by the media. Another was more forgiving. 'It's the nature of the job. If they don't look out for themselves, who will?'

When there was such intense competition for the same work, inevitably, swords would be drawn. Communication between peers was cautious and opaque. Information flowed through secret channels and any leaks could lead to another peer going for an audition and getting the job. The job was an efficient cleaver, neatly dividing one model from another with one clean swoop.

Trade unions, this lot had been taught in their neoliberal education, were never a solution; they were the problem. More practically, how would a union work? Who would operate it? Other solutions were offered, more in keeping with the times, the most prominent being affiliation with an international modelling agency.

—m—

The Agency was born in its current form in post war America with the setting up of Eileen and Jerry Ford's Ford Models in 1946. For years before this, licensed employment agencies (the most famous being the John Powers and Harry Conover agencies) managed models' assignments, taking cuts for the service. With Ford, there was a major shift.

Earlier agencies had not solved models' concerns, like late payments. Sometimes payment came a year, or even two years, after the job had been done. But Ford Models introduced a system of advance payment to their models that they later recovered from their clients. The idea for this system had come from a model herself.

Dorian Leigh, supermodel in the 1940s and 50s, had just left the Harry Conover agency because her clients couldn't get through to the phones at Conover, and hired herself a secretary to take her calls.[24] Other models started sharing the secretary. Leigh had just devised a 'voucher system' that could pay models as per their work done, when she met a young fashion stylist called Eileen Ford at a fashion photographer's office. Leigh's idea stayed with Eileen and came into practice when she and her husband Jerry, just returned from the war, started their agency in their apartment on Manhattan's Upper East Side.

At Ford, if you were one of 'their models' you got paid weekly, every Friday, without fail – less the agency cut, of course. Moreover, Eileen personally oversaw your development, gave dietary tips and shared beauty secrets, and even offered up their home for outstation models to sometimes stay in. Even though later Eileen admitted that this was a ploy to keep them under her watchful eyes so they would make it to early morning appointments, these strategies worked to make Ford Models the success they became: you take care of the modelling darling, their models were told, we'll take care of the business.[25]

Other agencies rose in competition but Ford continued to innovate with their next products: floating rates for models – negotiating prices according to the demand and supply around a model or a client, and then famously, modelling contracts. Not just any modelling contracts, but exclusive ones linking certain kinds of looks (models even) with specific brands. 'Their models' were now legally contracted for long periods to be 'the face of' something or the other, starting with Lauren Hutton's contract for Revlon in 1974. Payment for models went up exponentially as the power of branding came into force.

By this time, in New York alone, the modelling agency business was a $50 million one, and the stakes were getting higher. Former models (like Wilhelmina Cooper) had started agencies, including those who had been with Ford, but the real war started with the setting up of Elite Model Management in 1972 by John Casablancas, who had run an agency in Paris, even working with the Fords occasionally. Casablancas defied the unwritten rule of their working relationships that he would not set up a conflicting business in America. He also poached some of their best models and agents. What followed was high drama. Lawsuits worth millions of dollars, no-holds-barred sparring in the press, allegedly even a furious Eileen sending Bibles to the 'traitors' with passages on Judas marked in red.

In this period, agencies were embroiled in what was known as the model wars: poaching, cajoling, stealing lucrative models from one another; stoking egos and making certain models feel like a million bucks because well, sometimes that was literally what she was going to make them.

Models on their part ping-ponged from one to another and back to the first like children in a candy store, not sure which delectable extra offered by competing agencies would lead to the headiest sugar rush. They weren't just models anymore, they were the 'movie stars of the advertising industry' in the lingo of the agencies who tried to sell them exactly in that eulogized tone to their clients, extracting from clients the price of movie stars too. The agencies worked hard to make a lucrative 'supermodel' with good grooming, careful strategizing and crafty contracts, and many times that decade they did indeed hit the jackpot.

With the 1990s, modelling agencies could no longer remain local businesses. The big boys were now transnational corporate giants out to explore new markets and hungrily follow the trail of global capital. It wasn't enough to have an office in Miami, you needed to have offices or franchises in Kazakhstan and Venezuela for the real globalization experience. Agencies diversified and specialized. Smaller ones built themselves as boutique agencies, others specialized in catering to specific requirements: older people, young teens, body part models. But even as these frontiers expanded, relations between models and agencies were tenuous.

Too many contenders and a loss of interest on the part of agencies to cultivate the myth of the supermodel had slowed down the initial rush of supermodel mania. Eileen Ford herself recounted how they received over 10,000 letters every year but only three or four were really going to make it. Having suffered a burnout with some of their brightest stars (and deaths, drug scandals, lifestyle related illnesses, among them a high number of lung cancer cases) agencies were cautious in how they related to models. No more for them the movie-star treatment (although the lament of the agencies was, 'they don't make girls like they did anymore'). That bubble had burst.[26]

Agencies were also beset with other problems: takeovers, mergers, selling out, even bankruptcy. Elite Models, in fact, filed for bankruptcy in 2004 on the trail of other issues: allegations of sexual misconduct against top management, a hostile work environment and accusations of price fixing and manipulation of rates in the industry over lunches with other major agencies, as alleged by a lawsuit endorsed by 10,000 models.[27]

The 'agency model' took care of many of the models' business needs, but dictated too much of their lives. But these disgruntled murmurs by models were mere flies buzzing around their ear for the agencies, to be swatted away. The age of supermodels was over and the whimsy of clients was something newer, something younger, something fresher, and sometimes, something just a little exotic. The crawl of agencies over the world's map continued.

—m—

'I think we do the work of a union,' says Sushma Puri, Elite India's director and CEO at the time, a middle aged woman who had been a chartered accountant in London for many years. 'If I talk for the models, (our presence) has organized them. It's made sure that they get their payments. It's made sure they don't get exploited.'

Elite India was started in 2003 as a franchise of Elite Model Management International. Fifty models joined the agency at the end of their first year in India. By the end of the second year this had grown to 140 models, almost a 300 per cent increase in one year.

Elite didn't allow its models to work independently or with any other third party coordinators and took (at the time) a 30 per cent commission per job. In exchange, it ensured that payments were made to the models for work done within two weeks (unheard of in the industry apparently). 'The bad debt risk is ours. People are more wary about not paying a company and more so a company like ours, because they feel they will need to use us over and over again,' says Puri.

They also manage their models' appointments, market them to clients and oversee assignments with written agreements that profess to protect models' interests. They have a simple booking form that clients have to fill and sign, 'whether they like it or not' Puri says strictly. Contracts are regarded with suspicion in the industry, so this form is its cousin twice removed, a not-really-contract document that specifies the usage of the photo or the ad being contracted for, including territorial rights, the range of media, the period of usage, financial commitment and 'other conditions like protection of modesty and so on'.

What happens if someone who said they would only use the photo on billboards in Delhi also used them on buses in Baroda?

'They get slapped with another invoice if they abuse the terms,' says the director with a calm smile, quite the iron fist in a velvet glove.

They also offer to young models, the promise of protection. Like sheltered children, their models will never have to really worry about getting their hands dirty by going out into the real India and having to market themselves. 'With us, they don't get into…you know, sleazy kind of situations. When there's a casting happening and we're not sure about a client or if we are working with that client for the first time, we tell them to come here to the office and do the casting. If we don't have a comfort level with the client, then we won't send our girls, or boys for that matter.'

Elite was able to grow quick roots into the Indian scenario by shrewdly identifying and acting on India-specific concerns. One of them being parents. 'I think it's very specifically an Indian, or maybe South Asian, problem,' Puri says.

'Not just (parents)…but the extended family playing a very important role in a decision like this (joining the industry, or what kind of work to do). Trying to change the mindset of Indian parents has been the biggest challenge. I meet them all, the parents who come here. If they are below 21 their parents have to sign the contract. If the parents are not available to sign that contract, we don't take that person. Parents have questions; some have inhibitions about letting their daughters do certain kinds of work, which we take into account. This is because modelling, before we came in, was not looked upon too well. We've tried to change that image… make sure that people do feel that it's clean.'

Having thoughtfully gotten the pesky parents out of the way then, Elite also positioned itself carefully, straddling the identity of a professional business and in keeping with the India model of business, a 'family', very much modelled on protection by an indulgent patriarch – or in this case, a la Eileen Ford, a matriarch.

The director sighs, 'It's a huge responsibility to be in charge of such young adults. It's very stressful. In my mind what I wouldn't want my daughter or son to do, I wouldn't send these kids to do either.'

You would think she was talking about a convent school and not a modelling agency. Parental consent, check. Clean image, check. Suitable for middle class, check. Family values, check. Elite's understanding of the centrality of parents and the idea of family in the fields from which they will pick their flowers, the Indian urban upper and middle classes, has held them in good stead. The director hasn't forgotten why Elite is here in the first place. 'I think I give a lot of comfort to parents walking in because I am their age. We can talk about kids on the same wavelength. But essentially it is a business.'

—m—

'Why do I need an agency?' Noelle asks me before pressing the On button on her mixie. She's making cold coffee for us that hot April afternoon in her charming Gurgaon apartment with the walls she painted herself. One of the classic beauties of the modelling industry, Noelle is in her late twenties now, having modelled, been in music videos and even offered an item number, for well over a decade. She has lived through the models' union experiment as well as the agency hysteria.

For a minute I misunderstand her question. It's not 'why do I need an agency' but 'why do *I* need an agency'. As an older and successful model (even a 'senior') Noelle isn't really looking for help in getting her work or protection from the big bad wolves. It's a little late in the day for that.

Noelle pours out the chilled coffee into tall glasses as she answers her own question. 'If they come up with a better offer – like guaranteeing me a certain amount of money in a year or something like that – I might consider it. They will benefit by having me, I will get no extra benefit by being with them. Otherwise you are just branding for the agency.' And like her, the older generation of models feel there is hardly any incentive to join an agency like Elite, unless they are looking to change their area of work (say from print to TV) and starting as a newbie in a fresh field.

Noelle isn't going to give her hard-earned name to an agency to appropriate. For many like her, the work they put in to manage their own business is fairly invisible but to associate with an all-powerful agency would just undermine this. 'But for newcomers yes, agencies work,' she nods, passing me my glass. 'You don't have to go through the shady things like meeting people, calling them, doing the rounds and all that. When you're young, people manipulate you, abuse you, take you for a ride. So they need an agency, not us.'

The biggest recruitment base for agencies is, in fact, newcomers. Or models who have discovered after doing the rounds that there is no other option but seek the 'backing' of the agency. Tina is one of them. Coming from a wealthy industrialist family from South Delhi, she pooh-poohed the agency option but within months had to eat humble pie.

'I wasn't with Elite initially, I just joined them couple of months back. They had contacted me once, but I thought I could do it without them. Then as I was freelancing I realized it was really tough. So I came back to Elite, met Aunty and told her that I had made a mistake and I wanted to join them. She was nice enough to take me back. She's really motherly... This place is a good experience. And you know you have the correct backing.'

The correct backing is an important thing to have in the industry, and it's a lesson young people learn very quickly. But another benefit of an agency like Elite is that it establishes 'class'. By providing a physical space, their models feel that they can treat the agency premises as their 'office' and hold meetings and shoots in its plush air-conditioned interiors. 'I mean look around you, look at the office!' Tina waves her hand around the room we were sitting in for the interview. 'It's a place where you can ask people to come and meet you. It's a different feeling than going to 10 different coordinators in dingy dark alleys in Malviya Nagar.' For many aspiring models, this is also where they bring their parents to 'show' them their chosen occupation is legit, conducted from a real office.

The name itself, 'Elite', suggests a successful climbing of the social ladder. Through membership, aspiring models are able to transcend their class identities by belonging to this set of 'Elite models'. Tina is not friends with her co-workers, especially the ones from backgrounds different from hers, but she recognizes some sort of bond. 'There's a family feeling with Elite. We stick up for one another.'

Even though an agency like Elite is inclusive in its own way – it doesn't discriminate on the basis of class or background, as long as it makes good business sense – it divides models in the industry into agency/non agency groups, each with its own politics, scuttling any possibilities of collective organizing or unity between the two groups.

Elite also has other goodies to wangle in front of hungry youngsters seeking entry into the club: their global profile, and their ability to strong-arm the prices of models. By being an international agency, they offer opportunities abroad, still every young model's dream job and an important way to negotiate respectability with suspicious relatives.

Since 2005, a few more international agencies have come to India. The agency provides some sort of a new framework for the industry to conduct its affairs, but it is still not ideal.

'They make you do crazy things at shoots – climb a fountain, rock, anything! You could fall and break your head...so insurance should be in the contract,' Roopali pointed out. Even though Roopali was a star at her agency, she wasn't under any health insurance or safety cover given by the agency. Another young model with the agency suggested that comp cards (photo CVs of the models) should be an expense undertaken by the agency, instead of the model having to pay up to 5,000 rupees to the agency to procure comp cards every once in a while. Maternity leave, it was felt, should be given by the agency, 'if the model has been with an agency for a long period of time' being the caveat. But the most resounding ayes came for a more emotive right, an affirmation of intent: a 'commitment from the agency to take up cases of sexual harassment and other issues'. Models associated with an agency risked losing their autonomy: a non-negotiable for many fiercely independent models of previous generations.

For those outside the agency system, conceptualizing what rights they could have was even more difficult. Who would be the 'giver' of these rights? Who would these demands be made to? Still, words tumbled out: a minimum level of remuneration given the fragile nature of work in the industry; written contracts; written codes of conduct for the industry; overtime, and a complaints cell to report harassment, non payment or any other disputes.

Some ideas seemed ludicrous at first: a pension fund? Annual leave? But some models who had seen friends or colleagues with agencies abroad were less cynical. Roopali noted, 'My friend Liliana who I met in Shanghai is with this agency in Brazil, and they have an 11 month fixed contract. The year is planned ahead for them – they have to spend two months in Milan and so on… and after those 11 months they are entitled to 30 days annual leave. Here there is nothing like that.'

For both groups (those within an agency and those outside it), they still hadn't found an ideal situation. The choice to join an agency or not was the only real one on offer: the devil or the deep blue sea. Some joined the former and some jumped into the latter, confident that they would, some day, learn to swim.

CHAPTER NINE

Osmosis

I met Palash late one night in a coffee shop in Malviya Nagar. It was 9.30 pm and this meeting had come after being stood up twice. Sensing my dismay when I called her after the second no-show, she offered to meet me in 15 minutes at the coffee shop round the corner from her home, coincidentally also round another corner for me.

According to my notes of the meeting she came 'dressed most conspicuously, in a pink halter neck dress, mauve bustier inside, spindly knees, long legs, red football boots. She was wearing some make-up, eyes quite heavily done up'. With her close-cropped hair and pointed chin, she looked like a pixie in a manga comic.

Palash was frank at the outset, telling me we had to have some coffee or something otherwise they would not let us sit here. So we had coffee and duly tussled for the bill before settling down.

Palash's language was at odds with her appearance. Many of the girls from non-English medium schools had the beautiful bumblings of Indian English, or 'their own English'. Then there were those like Mayuri who were more intent on communicating, whatever the language, making no bones about dependence on her English-Hindi dictionary.

But with Palash it was different. Palash stubbornly refused to speak with me in Hindi – an option I had placed on the table at the outset – until the interview was formally over, and toiled over her answers valiantly in pop idioms and Americanisms picked up from TV, and here and there.

Palash's family was from northern Uttar Pradesh, a village that she had visited only three times since her birth. She had been born and raised in Kolkata in a modest, 'middle class' she stresses, upper caste home. Her father worked in a medical company, her mother was a housewife and she was the eldest of four children – the others all boys. 'They are very proud of me,' she adds, 'Whenever they see my photo anywhere, they get very excited.'

Her story was set in the regular mould: an ambitious boyfriend who sent in her pictures to Miss India, resistant parents, rebellious youth, a patron designer from her home city who was on the verge of launching into international design fame, a win at an international modelling contest and an assignment to model in Paris. Palash was not one for details, and what she told me was sketchy in every sense of the word.

'I was 18 and a half when I won the Model contest after finishing school. Mostly I was always looking at other people or practising like that in front of my boyfriend, just walking and posing for fun, watching on TV all the fashion channels and magazines, and learning from there. First time I was so nervous, there were all big big names and I was keeping quiet. Then the choreographer told me, "Your walk is excellent baby, you are great, don't worry, just go out there and do it." It was awesome. So like that it happened. Then I went to Paris after winning the contest and was doing shows abroad, everywhere I have gone so many places. I've done shows there for big designers.'

There doesn't seem to have been a period of struggle, I offered.

'No never, touch wood!', she shook her head vigorously. 'Straight only I went to Paris and did work in abroad. With contest there was no struggle period. Also you have to choose brand correctly. You have to avoid seedy choreographers, you know, things like that.' The contest wasn't her first attempt at entering the fray. 'Before that I tried for Miss India, and I was chosen as a finalist also! But I had family problems and my parents did not allow me to go to Bombay alone for the contest. They said I was too young to go on my own.'

She skims over details of her family and home, but makes just the right I-miss-my-family sounds. 'I travel back to my home in

Kolkata whenever possible. Even when I get three days I go to see them and be with my family and friends there. Otherwise yes there is some travelling for work. Its depend.' Work is what Palash really wants to talk about: ramp, print... 'No, I have not done any TV yet. And please don't ask me about films! I do not want to do films or item numbers so don't ask! Everyone asks this.' And Paris. 'Like I went to Paris. I got to know the profession from different way, in a more professional way. There it is just like a profession. Proper, everything is done through agencies, it is punctual. If you are not with an agency you cannot work as a model. Simple. If you go abroad you know so much more and that makes you better. Everyone will also know, oh she was modelling for Dior or something, and then you will be more established.'

Palash has her own ideas of what her job entails and is articulate about its nuances. 'In fashion our job is basically to show clothes, not to be oomphy or something like that. And it's depend, only some clothes are like that...and it's also depend on the designer. Anyway in India designers do not design too revealing clothes. They cannot because they know that it is different here. We have to make anything look good. See skin show is also an art. You have to carry it off, even if you go nanga you have to carry it off.'

The interview ends on a surreal note. Switching to Hindi the minute I flip the notebook shut, Palash wants to talk. Talk, as in talk-talk. What do you think about the spiritual, she asks me? Why do birth and death occur? I admit that these things do not occupy my mind frequently. Palash has strong opinions on religion and spirituality, the body and soul, the power of the mind, and feels people don't die unless they really want to and if they have something in their mind, some unfinished business. She gives me the example of an old man whose dream it is to build his own house. 'Only after he finishes does he die the day the house is made.' The waiters at the coffee shop interrupt us with an obvious cough. Even coffee shops must close.

Despite the two hour-long conversation that went almost into midnight, there were things about the interview that worried me. In my notebook, a scribbled note stands out. 'She was possibly not entirely honest about various things.' The fear of being fed lies or what the respondent thinks you want to hear, is always there at the back of a researcher's mind, but in Palash's case, there were some concrete reasons to suspect the authenticity of her claims – like claiming she did her graduation by correspondence, but also went to Paris on an international modelling contract, both of which seemed to be at the same time. Or her difficulty in reading the form I asked her to fill out, and asking me to fill it up for her, muttering excuses for being unable to read it properly. An illusion of being wealthy, but not having the cash to pay a 98 rupee bill. Speaking of a 'boyfriend' through the interview and then mentioning that she was actually married. Insisting she was part of Fashion Week but not being on the official list (perhaps she had been brought in only for the show of her mentor?). So much didn't add up.

Though I was bound by tradition to document every small detail, my notes in retrospect seem unkind in their replication of her speech. An arrogance at her language stares up from them, a faint cringe here, a stifled laugh there, a silent judgment between the lines. Perhaps I was exhibiting a prejudice common to the Indian middle class – to look down at people who we secretly believe are exceeding their brief. That they are trying to ridiculously (and in vain) 'class' themselves. That they are crossing limits and trying to move into a social set not 'meant' for them.

But let me return to tell you about others who moved not just from village to city or suburbs to centre, but attempted an osmosis of sorts. Those who travelled across borders – geographical and social – to inhabit and experience what it means to be elsewhere.

—∾—

1990. In a shopping mall in outer Toronto, a 16 year-old girl of obviously Indian origin was out with her family, when she was 'spotted' by a scout in a modelling agency. The scout approached the tall striking young lady and introduced herself as a booker for a local agency that managed local talent. She left her card with the surprised girl, telling her to call her if she wanted to ever think about modelling. Her height, according to the scout, was ideal.

Her reasonably progressive parents were sceptical of a future in modelling. This was a Western game for Western people and brown girls, however tall, didn't seem to stand much of a chance. Harsimranjeet, or Leher as she was locally known, agreed with her parents: it was true. There were hardly any girls from her Sikh community or Indian girls in general in the Toronto modelling scene. So she went along with the natural course of events: college, then a job as a business manager in a retail company. But the memory of that meeting remained.

Why not, she decided one day, toying with the card she had put away carefully. Why not? She called the scout, went to meet her, and on her advice got some pictures taken and agreed to do whatever came up next. She would do it part time.

'My first job, uh, I don't even remember it very well!' Leher reminisces. 'What I do remember is the fear: I was petrified that I would trip and fall. And the blinding lights on my face, I couldn't see a thing. I think it was a hair show on the ramp. I didn't really know anything. They don't have time to teach you there! You learn on the job.'

She did about two shows a month, and made some extra money from the gigs, getting about $80 to $190 (Canadian) an hour depending on the client or type of work. Soon she outgrew her small local agency. But getting a new agency was more difficult than she had thought. The ones she shortlisted and called 'already had one Indian girl' on their rolls and couldn't see the scope for another. The ideal Indian girl in these agencies was also of a certain kind targeted at South Asian audiences – big-busted, small waisted, small hips – far from her fit, athletic build.

A year or two later, Leher tried again. This time, there were more openings for Indian girls who met the standard Toronto model requirements – a straight up 'minimum height 5 feet 9 inches and body size 3 or 4', and Leher got snapped up by a large well known agency, who sent her to Montreal to audition for a major contract with an international cosmetics company. Leher got the account.

She was still doing this part time, having continued with her full time job. She would work eight hours, go for auditions during lunch break downtown where her office also was, shoot often for night shifts, go home, change, have tea and be back at work the next morning.

'I was a hard worker,' Leher blushes in explanation, 'For me two days work back to back was no big deal. And it paid off. The work and clients started getting better, the money went from two digits to three to four digits. I became a familiar face at auditions.' It wasn't just her who was juggling work. 'There, most girls aren't just models, they're also students, waitresses, whatever. They're all doing something else.'

As she became one of the 'top three show girls' in the city, she finally decided to model full time, and gave herself one year to really make it big. New York was the next logical step so always the cautious prepared one, she made a recce visit to the mecca of the North American fashion world. Two hectic days of rounds of 14 agencies later, she came back without landing any contracts.

'Someone suggested I go to India,' she says, 'You have the height they said. So I booked a ticket, and ironically enough, on the way to the airport, an agency from New York called me to say they were interested! But I think I had already decided to give India a try.' It was 2001 and things were changing in the Indian modelling world too, with international agencies stepping into the ring.

'I stayed with relatives in Delhi and met an agent. She was a great individual but very busy. No time for a one-to-one, and left me with her staff. I was very unhappy; it was disorganized and I felt I was wasting my money and time.' For Leher, the agency had always been her ally in the business, and things in Toronto had been so different from Delhi. 'In Toronto you have to have a good rapport with your agent or booker. It's a relationship thing; they go a long way to cover your back. My agent has even told me to walk out on clients who don't respect us or our time and keep us waiting forever.'

So Leher, on the advice of the gaggle of girls she had awkwardly befriended backstage, turned 'freelancer'. She moved out of her relatives' home and took up a place ('with really low rent') in Defence Colony with a Sikh couple as landlords who treated her 'like a daughter'. Her new life began.

In four months she became a known face, and in another two she became premium material. 'I just did what I did in Toronto,' she says thinking about what it was that made it so easy for her to become popular. 'I was professional, and treated people equally – things which are not done here. When I came I already "looked like a model" which seems to be important here. So half my work was done already.'

We are now sitting very far from Toronto and her life of the NRI model.

We are sitting in a living room filled with middle class memorabilia in a flat in a cooperative housing society in Sarita Vihar, having requested the aunty across the landing to look after her ten-month old toddler while we finish the interview. The aunty is very impressed and not a little intrigued that her neighbour is giving 'an interview' and quickly agrees to help, keeping her own questions for later.

'So what happened,' I ask her, 'when did you stop?' She is still. 'Modelling has a different reputation here than it does abroad. I didn't realize it till I fell for this guy from a traditional family. I was in total la-la land with him when I figured that being from this industry was a no-no. If I had known, I wouldn't have come.'

Leher's mother-in-law had been aghast at the turn of events in her son's life, swooning and raging alternately at the idea of a 'Canadian model' bahu. But the couple plunged zealously into the exhausting cycle of placating and pleading with family and relatives, won their battle and got married. 'My height was such an issue!' laughs Leher, 'Everyone wanted me to only wear flats after my wedding.' An unexpected pregnancy followed, and four months into it, Leher 'quit cold turkey'. 'I went out of sight out of mind. I didn't want to play the waiting game and wonder what was going to happen. And in this business once you've destroyed it, you can't go back.' She reins in the despair before it engulfs her, and I restrain myself from reaching out and hugging her.

Instead, we brush the remains of her grief under the dusty carpet and begin to rage about the eccentricities of the Indian modelling world, compared to the West. Why would they want to shoot for fur coats in the peak of summer at 40 degrees C?

Why does a ramp show take up three days of your time here, as opposed to not even one full day there? Why does everyone think I'll jump into a bikini just because I came from Canada? Why does a shoot for shawls involve wearing bikinis? Why does nobody have a backup plan here? Don't they know it's an uncertain business? Every model has a Plan B in Canada. Why do people here look at you differently? Why do people come to see parts of the body and not the show? Why do they give us dabbas for meals that fill your stomach with gas? Why do agents ask models strange questions: can you swim, dance, skate – dance while skating or skate while dancing? Do you have tattoos? Where? Do you have scars? Where? Where do you live, my dear?

'It wasn't like I wasn't Indian enough in Toronto,' she smiles. 'My mum would pack me a tiffin box every day. My brother would come with me "for safety", like when I auditioned for some music video. I would have to keep checking in at home by calling my parents every few hours. And raised in an Indian home, I wasn't comfortable showing any part of the body. The first few shows I would run into washrooms to change, or change behind racks but then I realized no one's looking at you!'

But working in India had been completely different. First, there was all the dressing up for meeting agents and clients. 'There, the only thing that gets you work is the book. You go to meet people as natural as possible, no contact lenses, no mini, no make-up, no stilettos.' Then there were the ways of working – the delays ('If you show up on time all you'll see are locked doors. There, 3 pm means you show up at 2.45 pm. My agent told me once "You can be replaced in a heartbeat".'), rate fluctuations as if divinely ordained ('There, I had to give 3 months advance notice that I was raising my rates! Here it happens overnight!'), the chaos backstage.

'There, you just bring yourself – unlike here when the choreographer will call you at some strange hour and tell you to bring golden shoes, beige bra, whatever. There you are told how to walk just before you go on to the stage. When you get in on your cue you are given the accessories or sunglasses, you walk, leave the stage, and someone is there to take it all off or back. You can't put anything on the floor, on the RACK ONLY. Not here – people just dump things anywhere, pile stuff on the floor and the helper does everything. Everything is in writing and the 20 per cent agent's commission is above your fee and goes straight from the client to the agent.'

Finally there was the obsessive gymming that everyone was into. 'There, people have no time to go to the gym. They're very active generally. And I guess they watch what they eat… Maybe that's why eating disorders are more common there,' she reflects. 'Here, a fair amount of time and energy is spent in manicures, pedicures, facials, going to a parlour. Unthinkable back home.'

Leher did a show a few weeks ago, her first since the baby. And she was pleasantly surprised by the affection showered on her baby boy by the ladies backstage. 'It was such a different experience. They were all helping out without even being asked…' Is she going to go back into the ring, I ask? Leher shrugs and gets up. It's probably time to get her little fellow back, I reckon. But she goes inside and brings out a black album. 'Would you like to see my book?' she asks. Sure, I say, and we squat on the carpet to look into the past, opening up the black folder as an avalanche of glossy photos happily tumble out.

―∞―

Going West was a lucrative dream to have – for the doctor, for the software engineer, and later for the investment banker. But for a model? No quotas were being set out in immigration policies for them, but prior examples even sparse, had shown that going westwards to model could bring global stardom.

The seventies were abuzz with the story of a tall, dark, gawky girl who had faced rejection in the Indian modelling industry but defiantly gone to Paris and pretended to be a princess to get an appointment with Pierre Cardin, and charmed him at sight. Phyllis Mendes was her name, but she went by the more exotic Anjali Mendes. This was by different accounts either a clever take on 'a jolie' ('oh pretty' in French), a term of endearment Pierre called her by or a shortened form of Gitanjali, a name suggested by her friend, the Paris correspondent of *Times of India* at the time,

Dileep Padgaonkar. Mendes became Cardin's muse for twelve years, but in pop folklore remained 'the Goan girl who served sorpotel with champagne in her Parisian apartment'.[28]

Another instance followed soon. She was a Parsi girl from Bombay, and her name was Persis Khambatta, who at 17 had won the Miss India title, but turned down the role of playing the Bond girl when she went to participate in the Miss Universe pageant because she had promised her mother she wouldn't be tempted by any such offers. Two years after her pageant win, she was cast in a Hindi film called 'Bambai Raat Ki Bahon Mein' where she played Lily, a nightclub singer in a blonde wig. Her unremarkable Indian stint onscreen was in stark contrast to the fame she found almost 10 years later as she went where no Indian woman had gone before, as the bald Lt. Aliea in the sci-fi cult Star Trek enterprise. By 1980, she earned a place in quizzing trivia when she became the 'first Indian ever to be called on to present an award at the Oscars'.

These shooting stars came sporadically, without any real logic or announcement, and so remained in the domain of luck by chance. But in the mid-2000s, with Indian self-confidence at a new high, it seemed like luck was on our side, as India's standing in the international arena appeared to broaden its chest.

The benchmark at the time was a Maharashtrian girl, Ujjwala Raut, about whom the Indian press wrote that she was a shining example of how the West was now ready for Indian talent. The buzz around Ujjwala continued as the media followed her as she received modelling offers for high-end fashion shows, a contract as the face of an international luxury brand, and for becoming part of a charmed circle of creative, wealthy and artistic people, so much so that in 2004 she got married at rockstar David Bowie's home in New York with his wife and her best friend Somalian born model Iman as witness. Around then, a handful of Ujjwala hopefuls made flight to go West, and ride on the possibilities that seemed to suddenly abound. Of these were Naina, Mita, and Anupriya.

Naina was an established model in Delhi, muse to many an edgy designer. Naina had started modelling in the mid-nineties straight out of school. She had won the May Queen ball, a contest for defence personnel and their families, when she was 16. That was where she met a choreographer duo who took a special liking to her and a lifelong association with them was born. For Naina, modelling seemed to be marginally more exciting than classes in a girls' college. She became a staple on the fashion scene, and for the next few years was the rage. Then, boredom struck.

In an effort to up her game, Naina tried to wade into newer waters: Paris. 'It's quite a landmark if you model abroad,' she nods, twirling her foot, with nails painted black, encased in a golden kolhapuri chappal. 'Getting to Paris is very easy to do. Or to get an agency to take you. What's tough is what comes after that and what you have to do the next few years.' What did she have to do that was so tough? Naina shifts onto the other hip and languidly pulls up her feet under her.

'Look. Here I don't have to go for castings. There, I was brand new so I had to go everywhere for auditions. The agency pays for your accommodation, food, portfolio, everything. So they have to make sure that you do an X amount of jobs so they are reaping the money they have invested in you. Here I can choose to work when I feel like, I can choose to say no. But out there when you are starting out, you are their slave! If you are one pound overweight, they MAKE SURE that you lose weight in the next two days. They sell you. You're a commodity for them.'

Naina returned to India at the end of the season, wanting to quietly slip back into her top-model coat quickly before it passed onto a newbie. She shrugs nonchalantly, 'I was very happy to come back. I didn't have the patience or the inclination to stick it out. I didn't see myself working THAT hard towards something I see as fun.'

For newbies like Mita and Anupriya who had just started out in the industry when they 'went international', the 'tough times' were worse. Mita was already with a global agency's franchise in India two years into her career when an opportunity arose. Mita is dressed to the gills as we sit for the interview in a deserted classroom used for modelling classes at the agency. She is to shoot something for a news channel next. 'One of my friends is friends with the owner of an agency in the USA. That man was in India for a day on his way to Shanghai. My friend called me and said why don't you just come in and meet him, he is also here to look for girls and take them to Ecuador for an in-house contest, and then onward to New York.'

New York was for her an 'eye-opener'. 'Suddenly I was out of this little world of mom and dad, fun and parties and thrown into a very fast paced world. Nobody has time for you.'

Mita was, by Indian standards, very thin when she went, but the expectations from the agency were clearly different: in Mita's word, they wanted a look that was 'anorexic, that is like really, really thin. Like a 13 year old girl. The agent told me, till the time you don't lost weight you can't do any jobs.'

Mita stuck around even as the grim realities of living alone in New York City crept up on her every day. Her friend's friend was busy travelling the world and her interaction was now only with his cold, unfriendly staff – 'the agency' – a far cry from the homely aunty and friendly bookers who would party with her back at her 'mother agency' in Delhi.

The agency told her soon enough they couldn't give her an apartment as it was a lean period for them. 'They did not give me any cash and you know after four months and being there… I skipped meals because I did not have enough cash, I walked because I did not have money for the metro. It was difficult but it taught me a lot of things. Taught me a lot of humility. In India everything is different. Seems like I took it for granted.'

The little work she got showed her how different modelling in New York was from New Delhi. 'Every girl has a make-up artiste and hairdresser backstage, not one for the whole show like here. They are paid by the hour, 200 dollars an hour. In a show, everything is taken into consideration – the colour of your skin to the length of your hair to the colour of your eyes. It is a very different world.'

Mita exited quietly, having had enough as winter came. 'I was there from August till November. It was crazy, I didn't have proper clothes, I took coats thinking it's like Delhi in winter.' She returned to the warm embrace of her agency in Delhi, much thinner, but ready and hungry to work her way through the local scene.

For Anupriya, the opportunity to be the next Ujjwala Raut came knocking at exam time when she was chosen as the winner in an international modelling contest. It had barely been six months since she had started modelling, winning the odd contest in her native town Guwahati, and plugging in to the Miss North East current that flowed from the seven sisters states to Delhi, where she had been sent by her doctor parents to do her graduation in a posh women's college. This big contest brought opportunity knocking on her door, mistimed as it was, forcing her to choose between a graduation degree or an international modeling career. Anu chose the latter.

'I had to leave my studies because the contract said that I had to go to Paris from January till April, which is when the college exams are here. It was a difficult choice because I went against my parents. They were like wait for three-four months then you can do it. But that is not in my hands you know. They wouldn't have called me again. Because it doesn't work like that there.'

That decided, the next challenge was to shape up. 'I was little heavy that time, heavy on the hips. So I was on diet for at least a month, because they told me you have to lose weight, otherwise we can't take you there.'

'They specifically told me, if you can reduce weight from arms it's fine, otherwise hips is going to be too broad – it was 38 and they wanted 35. And they told me can you please reduce three kilos also. So I was on boiled food, kaccha paneer and all that. It was like a shock because I had only two weeks to lose weight. I told the person who was grooming us – another top model – I don't think I will be able to do it, because I was used to eating chicken and fish, being an Assamese. But she said: look at Ujjwala, where she is now and even you have to be. You have to do it. So I did it, but it was difficult.'

Along with the diet came a strict gym routine. Did it all work, I ask? 'Ya it worked,' she laughs. 'Completely. I felt asleep you know but people used to tell me that you are looking so different because my face changed.'

Anu's first time in Paris was beset with minor issues. 'I don't know how to speak French. The first time they sent me for some casting, I got lost. For six hours I was just walking up and down. It was raining so I was all wet, I was crying, it was like a hell for me.' Then there was the hard work. 'Life is so hard there, every morning nine o'clock you had to take the lists from the casting people and we used to go for at least 10 castings a day. And you have to complete the full 10. And, well, they never told me that I had to take care of my own expenses. Apartment I had to pay, and it is not like in rupees, it is in euro, and food I had to pay, rent also. I was staying alone because my booker told me it is better if you can stay alone, because in model's apartment a lot of things happen. It is not safe blah blah blah.'

Luckily for Anu, one after the other, she hit bulls eye at the relentless castings and the financial worries began to smoothen out. She enjoyed her new found independence, never having been one for too much family. 'I always wanted to live alone, so it is like a dream come true again. So I never missed my home or my family as such.' As the season finished and she returned to Delhi in the summer – now a 'promising international model', she saw how much the outing had done for her career. Not only was she now 'foreign returned' and therefore more precious with a presumed international network in the global fashion world, she was also able to, for the first time, command her price.

'Paris was the turning point,' she agrees when talking about rates. 'Initially, I didn't have any right to decide. But after the Paris trip I found that whatever money I was getting here was like peanuts! Money was so good there, even after my agency saves 60 per cent from me so whatever 40 per cent I get was no comparison to India.'

Anu returned to India but has been back in Paris for a few seasons since, building on her hopes of being the next Ujjwala. 'This year when I went, my booker and I stayed with two gays for two weeks. They were very sweet, they treated me like a princess. They used to cook for me, put my clothes in the washing machine, and dry them too.' The tough times are behind her but she isn't moving there in a hurry, happy to bask in the glory of occasional ramp shows in Paris and Milan, but clear that she can be in both places at the same time. She's not done with the West yet.

—᙮—

It was years later when I found out that my fears were not unfounded, that there were many things Palash had not told me. That her real name was in fact not Palash at all, but Pushpa (but where was someone going to go with a name like that?). That she barely had any contact with her family anymore, that she came from a much more economically deprived background than she let on, in fact, a starkly poor family living in a one room tenement in a lower income by-lane where she would come once in a while and drop some money to help out. These I discovered perchance when she was in a freak accident that disfigured her, and newspapers in her home state picked up on the tragic story.

It wasn't only Palash who had constructed a life for me (perhaps, many elements true to some degree) to match a template that already existed: a sympathetic boyfriend, conservative upper caste parents, a traditional not-so-ambitious family-loving girl inside a modern fashionable exterior, given a break by one of India's most talented designers, a true professional familiar with the modeling scene in Paris, headed for greatness. With the internet quickly becoming the archive of our times, others continued to construct little details that changed from time to time. Anu went on to become an even more celebrated model, and garnered a fan following. On her website, suddenly she was able to rewrite elements of her past – her year of birth, for example, wherever mentioned did not match my records – to match her possibly shining future.

Another article came up a few years ago, a small side story in a regional paper that I caught while visiting the city. It was a phoenix rises from the ashes story littered with hyphens. About the once-famous, Paris-returned, rags-to-riches model Palash who had picked up the reins of her life after the tragedy, looked at her disfigured self in the mirror and overcome the odds to return to the only world she knew – the fashion world – in another role: as a stylist. Helped alongside by sympathetic model friends and a designer who had supported her all along.

It was, by all accounts, quite a story. That night I clinked a glass to the pixie woman I had met years ago in a coffee shop in Malviya Nagar who had confounded me with her contradictions, but also shown me a glimpse into the real possibilities of osmosis in a fragmented world.

CHANGE

Today's girls, if they join a contest and win it, they're not going to waste it. They're not going to get married and have kids at 22 like I did.

Meera, Miss India winner, 1970s

CHAPTER TEN

Curtains

When I was wrapping up my field work, I was eight months pregnant. Perhaps that was what brought the situation of models who chose to have children to my attention.

Shirin, top model during the late 1980s, told me how she had worked right through her pregnancy and never felt having children would mean she would lose out on anything. She says, 'I remember I shot for this whiskey brand and for a famous cold drink both when I was seven-eight months pregnant. They put me into this gown and I couldn't breathe! And every now and then somebody would unzip me and I would be on the set with this complete unzipped back and this stomach…!'

Shirin laughs at the memory. She is quick though to point out that she herself had a different approach to her pregnancy than many other Indian women.

'I swam and worked and did everything till my eighth month. I shot in this black dress. If you ever saw that film you would never know that I am pregnant at all. I was seven and a half months pregnant. I shot a soap ad in a tub, in a field full of flowers for four days with a huge belly… Everybody used to laugh every time I stepped out of the tub, and they would be like, gosh this is ridiculous!'

This matter-of-fact tolerance of women's changing bodies disappeared within the decade.

By the time Ritu's turn came to rule the advertising roost in the early 1990s, being pregnant, even notionally, became the beginning of the end of a career.

Did she have any fears about her body changing with the baby? She nods. 'I put on about 14 kilos during my pregnancy. But as I'd always been working out I knew I could lose weight even if I gained. But of course there were fears.'

Ritu felt betrayed that all the calls stopped even as people just heard her 'good news'. With just that piece of information, the industry wrote her off. 'Marriage did not make a difference, but after the baby, yes. I think people thought I would have become fat, out of shape, or just won't have time with a baby around.'

Ritu smiles, 'Strangely though motherhood made me thinner! Even though I was not fat, it didn't matter. People's perception is that once you have a baby, you sit at home. Only *you* know that you are perfectly capable, but others don't really want to know. And yes, you do go out of circulation for a while. The parties stop. You get that call occasionally – but that's it. Out of sight, out of mind, that's what happens. It's a very temporary profession anyway, either you're there or you're not.'

Ritu did her last show in her fourth month. 'Until then I was not showing, but in that show it was a little evident, people could see my belly then. After that show I stopped working. I stopped going out and being seen also. In this business if you are fat in the last show, you are fat forever in their minds! How they have seen you last is how they remember you. It's a looks based industry anyway. When I came I replaced people, so other people will replace you also. That's how it is.'

Ritu's daughter was then two. She had hired a PR agency to start getting some pictures of her out in the press and started attending industry parties in the hope that people would see that she was in shape and ready to resume work.

Twenty-nine year old Leher, who also stopped working in her fourth month in 2005 says, 'After having a baby you have to play the waiting game and just wait for people to realize that you are back in shape.' Leher was surprised when she was asked by a choreographer to model for a show when her baby was eight months old. It was her first show after becoming a mother and she was more nervous than ever before.

As it happened, Leher's baby sitter never showed up that day.

But Leher was determined to to do the show. So she decided to take her baby with her to the venue after consulting the choreographer. It turned out to be one of her best experiences of being in the industry. She recalled, 'It was wonderful! It was the first time I was seeing a different side to the models – all the other girls took turns at playing with him, they were all helping out without being asked, and they even left the room to smoke because the baby was in the greenroom. I really felt good about that show.'

That year, however, disturbing stories emerged in the media about the exacting requirements of having a perfect body, ideally an unchanging body. Even big hands, for example, were not acceptable. A film star allegedly was asked to use a 'hand double' (a 'hand model' to substitute for her hands) when she endorsed a jewellery brand during her pregnancy.[29] The hand model says, 'Since she was pregnant, her hands were big when she was shooting for the ad, and they couldn't use them.' During the shoot, the model sat on a low stool behind the actress and 'stuck (her) arms out underneath the star's shoulders, so that on camera it looked like they were hers.'

The tide is turning again, rising after the complete aversion in Ritu's time to a more tolerant one that Leher caught the crest of. With a celebrity baby boom in the last decade, many international and national celebrities have come into the spotlight, open about their pregnancy and experiences as a new parent. A visibly pregnant model Carol Gracias walked the ramp during Fashion Week in 2016 in a sari. The same year, Bollywood actor and star Kareena Kapoor walked the ramp for Fashion Week at the end of her pregnancy, and again within two months of having a baby. New role models include the ultimate 'yummy mummies' – the scores of women pop stars, music divas, film stars, social media darlings, those famous-for-being-famous, who have become mothers and remained 'in shape', labouring single-mindedly in gyms with personal trainers and following strict fitness regimes.

As a result, motherhood doesn't seem to be the death-knell to a modelling or acting career like it once was. But there are caveats and new, insistent pressures, underscored by social media as models are being photographed relentlessly (and voluntarily) all the time. Now women believe that one can return to the field, but the fine print says, this is possible only if they are able to return to their 'virgin' body – untouched by the natural effects of birthing. As if, former supermodel Niharika says wryly, 'time had stood still and nothing had happened'.

—⁂—

The average age of retirement for a model in the West is rumoured to be 26. Rumoured because no one really knows why and for what reason women in the industry have to call it quits or when it's time for the curtain to come down. Rumoured also because no one really knows how old the women are, age being such a closely guarded secret in the business. As if a number can control the fate of their career.

It does. You could look 21 but if you're known to be 29, you are unlikely to get audition calls. You could be 23 but if you look 30, there go your chances. The win-win combination is to look young – eternally – and to keep your age a secret by hiding behind charming clichés.

Shirin who is approaching 40 (maybe) and has recently modelled for an anti-ageing cream, feels that this idealizing youthfulness or maintaining a youthful body is not unique to the industry, but a general trend. The aggressive preservation and maintenance of youthfulness defines women of her generation today, as compared to previous generations of women who succumbed to 'being old' much too easily. 'I think fear of ageing has been a Western issue in the past. We, in India, are inherently not afraid of ageing. Here women especially age faster than they are supposed to. My mother will say, "Oh! My daughter is over 18, how will I wear long earrings?" How ridiculous! They came from a different generation.'

For Shirin, her generation is not like that. 'We are forever young. We do not ever want to be old,' she says with pride. 'If you look at me and five of my friends at an evening out…there have been times when we are standing next to the children and somebody has asked me, so are you in the same college with her?

We are aware of nutrition, vitamins, products, creams…we have 20 awarenesses! We are aware of clothing and how it best suits us, what we look like and how we should use it.'

Shirin points out how the role models for her generation are also older, well-maintained, successful women. She says, 'In my mother's generation if the children were teenagers, beti badi ho gayi then all is done. You gave up at 40. Today, at 40 you begin because finally by the time I am 40 my kids are going to boarding school or college.'

Life begins at 40 for Shirin and her well maintained friends but for a working model, it is certainly the end of her career. It doesn't matter as long as you look young, the girls would say hollowly, wanting to believe themselves. They would then give the example of Niharika, who had been modeling for decades but was still visible on the ramp. But Niharika was the only example they could find – and reluctantly they would cede that perhaps she was the exception.

Niharika herself is cautious about her continued presence on the ramp. She has seen her peers fall by the wayside. Even 'supermodels' who were barely 25, but suddenly one day stated to be 'past their prime'. What did it even mean, she says outraged, 'past your prime'?

'When you are cut off from this industry, it happens almost overnight,' she says grimly. 'And by overnight I mean over a couple of months. Suddenly you are not getting work because someone has decided that you're looking too old, too grey or too wrinkled… or you're just not it. And for no tangible reason! You couldn't have aged in just those six months! You couldn't have become "out" or not "hot" in six months. But someone – maybe some choreographer, or designer, or photographer, or just the media – has decided and made it applicable to you, and just cut you loose. And then they can be very, very cruel.'

'My friend, for example.' She takes a sip of water and shakes her head. 'She was such a supermodel. One of the country's finest. She is the same age as me, but she stopped modelling ten years ago. Initially she had all this media hype, because she was on top…but suddenly for whatever reason they started writing, saying, "oh she looks old, she's looking tired, she's got the same expression". My friend says she retired…but I think she was forced to retire because the media wrote so much against her. The criticism got too much.'

The outrage is back. 'Who judges whether the person has become old, or still looks young? In a government firm, you have 58 or 60 as the retirement age. Because they have considered that for the mental facilities to work that is the cut-off point. But here there is no such thing! Who is the one who draws the line? It becomes a very subjective kind of situation to be in.'

What's worse, according to Niharika is the way people forget shared journeys, how everything becomes water under the bridge. 'When your career ends I feel that is the biggest problem…to a certain extent even I have had a little bit of trouble dealing with, you know, The Chop. And how people forget – people you have done favours for, worked with, grown with.'

Niharika entered the industry when it was changing. The evolution had just started, she says, 'of turning from an entertainment into serious business.' She recalls, 'I started with a lot of designers who started out at the same time. We grew together. Today I've seen the attitudes changing, because maybe they have become huge as designers. And I realize that they don't value people. They've let themselves lose touch with reality, which I think this industry can do to people. You can lose touch with the fact that everyone is a human being.'

Niharika is silent. She says, 'I've been smart enough to do alternative things, and I'm still modelling so I haven't felt that (bad)…but I've seen other models in the past and felt really bad. And I've made an effort to keep in touch with them and make them feel… you know… that someone cares.'

The fear of ageing goes beyond a fear of wrinkles, it is to do with the end of a source of livelihood, the end of a lifestyle, an end over which the women themselves have little control. A young Nancy told me about the insecurity she lives with, 'My career can end today, tomorrow or next week if someone wants it to'. She wakes up every morning wondering if this will be the last day of her modelling career. Even those who may be at an age where they may have many work years in them, can face sudden and unwarranted 'expulsion' from the industry according to the whims and fancies of a more powerful person or medium.

How do women deal with this invisible pink slip? 'Some people become recluses, some people retaliate,' Niharika says. 'Some people just get married and kind of barely manage. Some people move on. And then there were some who I know couldn't give it up…and kept trying and trying and trying…saying "oh my weight must be the problem, I'll lose more weight" or "this must be a problem, I'll do that"… and you know not being able to LET GO. And I felt terrible. You know?'

Niharika gets much less work than she used to now, even though technically she is still modelling. 'But because I have other things to fall on I am able to deal with it, and I'm not talking about (family). Family and all that can help a little bit, it can't completely help you. Because the void is inside you. And work is work. You can't say, okay I have given up work because I have a child and my family and that is my priority. That's a different facet of life, which you can also do while work is happening. I am completely fulfilled when my child is around, but work wise I might still be feeling a nagging restlessness. I know I can take it easy now, so I am doing that…but it's not that I didn't feel that…anguish. There was anguish when the work stopped coming. It just didn't carry on that long.'

For the physical occupation that modelling is, it is mental resilience that will pull them through this final stretch.

Chapter eleven

A Short and Personal History of the Objectification and Commodification of Women

Feminism grew quietly on Indian shores.

Seeds sown in the 1940s and 50s with 'the women's question'[30] (on women's education, suffrage and social reform) flowered somewhat, as side patches along the margins of other social movements. Fresh buds sprang forth as women steered the anti price rise and Chipko movements in the early 70s, but it was only later that decade that the flowers bloomed ferociously, asking for a garden of their own: as the autonomous Indian women's movement.

Young women in city colleges reading of equality and civil rights, women returning from Western universities under the influence of radical feminist texts, those doing social work in rural India, those involved with left parties and civil liberties groups – all met serendipitously as a case of a tribal girl collided with their lives.

In 1979 a judgment on what was called the Mathura Case – the custodial rape of a young tribal girl named Mathura by two policemen – brought these women out into the streets. The court acquitted the accused policemen and stated that Mathura seemed accustomed to sexual activity, and thus could not have been 'raped'.

The judgment triggered massive agitations in the metro cities.

A group called Forum Against Rape was formed in Bombay, its members realizing in a moment of blinding clarity that other movements were not going to take up rape as a serious issue. They would have to look to one another to understand and empathize with Mathura and many like her.

'Mathura transformed us into feminists,' wrote Nandita Gandhi,[31] one of the early members of the Forum. Gandhi says of the time, 'We were enraged. The fear of rape is there within all of us. It was an emotional link for us as women.' The first protest march they took part in was 'like a catharsis' for the women: for the first time middle class women were out on the streets shedding their middle class demeanour and shouting slogans against rape.

The embers fanned into a fire as the many oppressions of women began to come out into the public domain. The Forum Against Rape renamed itself the Forum Against the Oppression of Women (FAOW). Dowry murders (till then called 'dowry deaths' and passed off as 'accidents'), the Bhopal gas tragedy, the Sikh massacre in Delhi: the 1980s created a whirlpool of outrage that spat out a series of radical feminist groups including India's first feminist publishing house (Kali for Women). With names that invoked feminine power, liberation, and sisterhood (Stree Mukti Sangathan, Stree Sangharsh, Saheli, Chingari), these groups (and many more, including seven new women's studies centers) became spaces for intense discussion and exploration of feminist ideas.

Gandhi recalls how they had to be constantly able to counter the arguments thrown their way. 'If we were told "only sick men rape", we had to be able to give a coherent argument for something we knew instinctively to be untrue,' she says. So cyclostyled readings were shared, debated, internalized and applied to local contexts. 'We felt connected to the world through these readings,' recalls Gandhi. 'All over the world, feminism was changing people's ideas.'

Debates on the objectification of women began within these groups through discussions on the representation of women in media. A study was conducted by *Manushi*, a newly set-up feminist magazine, on the content in three women's magazines (*Femina*,

Eve's Weekly in English and *Sarita* in Hindi) in the late 1970s. The authors of the study were of the view that the cover girls in these magazines were like 'dolls in a shop window' – the 'ideal women' of men's fantasies. The focus though was more on the mass media as a tool of ideological control, and the objectification argument (though not explicitly called that) took a back seat.[32]

The question of representation of women was one of the issues around which women's groups sought legislation in the mid 1980s, a period of significant legal reform that was driven by women's groups. The Indecent Representation of Women (Prohibition) Act 1986 was an attempt to prevent derogatory depiction of women in the media. Even as the law was being passed, activists were alarmed when the Chief Minister of Orissa at the time, J.B. Patnaik, called back an issue of the *Illustrated Weekly* for carrying a picture of a semi-nude woman, citing the new law. Feminist activists protested the magazine's recall, noting that the same issue also carried an expose of the Chief Minister, the real reason for the magazine's confiscation. The new law had been used as a decoy.

The experience made several women's groups question their own strategy of using the law as a way of preventing 'indecent representation' of women – but without really re-visiting what qualified something as being 'indecent' or 'obscene', a more commonly used word in censorship laws.

Two years later, another case came along that forced them to look at this question.

'Pati Parmeshwar' was a Hindi film released in 1988 about a devoted Hindu wife who submits dutifully to a philandering husband all because he is her lord ('parmeshwar'), her husband ('pati'). The censor board (Central Board of Film Certification) called for a ban on a film, citing that it had 'visuals or words depicting women in ignoble servility to man or glorifying such servility as a praiseworthy quality' – one of the things they were mandated to regulate. A Bombay High Court judgment overturned the ban and allowed the film to be released, with the judge, Justice S.C Pratap, saying the devoted wife in the film 'exemplified the inner strength of womanhood'.[33]

Feminists found themselves siding with the censor board,

and spoke out against the judge's glorification of servility. A new articulation of objectification emerged as feminist lawyers argued that the idea of the 'husband as lord', and 'ignoble servility' was the Indian form of objectification of women, rather than sexual objectification, as in the West.

—〰—

In the late 1980s and early 90s feminist groups were consumed by the politics waged on their bodies as wombs. They battled the perception of women in society as being essentially childbearing machines, with little say or choice in the matter. They fought campaigns against the population control politics of the Indian state (coercive sterilization of poor women and men to stem population growth, seen as the main obstacle to India's development),[34] against unethical trials of injectable and other contraceptives by pharmaceutical companies, upholding women's rights to have control over their bodies.

The feminist health movement engaged with the body more intimately, training women to know and love their bodies, to even look at them. Very few women had ever looked at their naked bodies in the mirror, such was the veneer of shame stitched fastidiously onto Indian women's bodies – even those of feminists.

Health activist N. Sarojini, then with Delhi-based group Jagori, recalled the challenge of practical sessions in their trainings that involved 'examinations of breasts, bimanual examinations of the uterus, abdominal examinations and so on'. Sarojini wrote, 'I was very hesitant initially and discussed this with Abha (Bhaiya, co-founder of Jagori, a Delhi based feminist group). She asked me once, "Don't you look at your face in the mirror? How different is that from looking at any other part of your body? Don't you let the doctor to examine you when you go to a clinic for any complaint?"'[35]

In those days, the most obvious expression of discomfort with objectification was in feminist responses to sexist ads, and occasionally the local beauty pageant. Members of the Bombay-based FAOW Nandita Shah and Nandita Gandhi remember protesting outside Shanmukhananda Hall in Bombay in the late 1980s where the Miss India pageant was being held. 'It was not that big, or prestigious at the time,' Shah says. They stood with other activists outside the venue with placards to mark their objection. Shah recalls, 'At that time, the contention was objectification. That women were being reduced to just their bodies like lumps of lard.' What did the placards say? Gandhi laughs. 'Ban the beauty pageant, what else! We had limited imaginations at the time, re!'

Across the country, groups turned vigilantes against sexist ads on billboards and film halls where 'blue films' were showing with posters of women in different states of undress. Women's groups learnt how to procure ladders, climb onto billboards to blacken them, how to throw tar or black paint so it would strategically hit the target (often pictures of women's body parts, being used to sell the product being advertised).

Feminist activist Madhu Bhushan, at the time with Bangalore-based group Vimochana, remembers an ad for Godrej typewriters that used the trope of the secretary as its theme. A buxom woman in a polka dot dress with cleavage showing, with the tagline 'The type you can click with'. 'We blacked it out, brought the hoarding down,' Madhu says. 'There was a funny backlash to our acts,' remembers Madhu. 'The hoardings were put back up with black bands on strategic parts, which made it more conspicuous!'

Kalpana Viswanath, a researcher and activist then working with Jagori, remembers protesting against a print ad for a chocolate biscuit by Brittania. The ad referred to the temptation of chocolate, with the tagline 'When women say no, they mean yes'. Kalpana was horrified by the message – coinciding as it did with efforts from women's groups against sexual assault, pointing out that 'no meant no'. She says, 'We mobilized other women's groups, and had it removed.' They wrote to the company registering their protest at the problematic line and its wider implications. Brittania withdrew the ad.

Several of the older feminists now remember that phase with some embarrassment. Madhu says, 'If you look back today it's almost like moral policing. Feminist moral policing.' 'We were uncomfortable to stand alongside the BJP (right wing) women. We were against objectification, but for them it was a moral issue,' reflect Gandhi and Shah, remembering how the group had gone blackening posters of *Blue Lagoon*, a Brooke Shields film with nudity, seeing it as semi-pornographic.

As feminist academic Mary John says of the time, 'We had confused sexism with showing of too much skin as a sign of domination and patriarchy. It was an incomplete argument.'

Concerns around body image overall were absent in that period. Queer feminist activist Jaya Sharma recalls returning from the UK after higher studies, and finding that the groundbreaking 'Fat is a Feminist Issue' by Susie Orbach had bypassed Indian feminists. She says, 'Elite class feminists have never been very political about the body. I would be mildly horrified how even the most vociferous feminist had no qualms saying "oh you've lost so much weight" or "you've put on weight", even though it might be in contradiction to our feminist politics.'

Comments from politician Mulayam Singh Yadav on short haired women 'parkati aurat' as he mocked his arch rival Mayawati after she got a 'bob-cut' riled feminists across the country, but that (and a critique of 'fairness') was the extent of engagement with body image.

It was only in 1993 that sexuality entered the conversation in a more robust way, when a Bollywood song snapped open a Pandora's box. Madhuri Dixit's bosom heaving sensuously in the song 'Choli ke peeche kya hai' ('what lies behind the blouse') from the film *Khalnayak* divided feminists nationally into those who thought this constituted vulgarity and objectification of the body, and those who thought this was an expression of female sexuality, even erotic in its delivery.

Such a division however disappeared as the Miss World pageant in 1996 brought Bangalore to a halt.

—ɷ—

On the eve of the international Miss World pageant in Bangalore in 1996, organized by Amitabh Bachchan Corporate Limited (ABCL), the city erupted in protest.

There were three 'parties' that were part of the protests, the Left, the Right, and the Left-leaning Feminists. All three were, in fact, protesting different things.

Left parties and their supporters were objecting to globalization's effects (as symbolized by the pageant). Right wing parties objected to Westernization and the erosion of Indian culture they felt this would lead to. And women's groups were protesting for a combination of reasons, including the 'commodification' of women. Rather than mere objectification (the premise of previous protests), the concerns this time were about women being a marketable commodity in the (then new) context of globalization in India.

The media and public however could not appreciate the nuance. The perception remained that the fracas was moral opposition to women going onstage in a bikini. (The organizers later 'solved' the problem by shifting out the swimsuit round to the Seychelles Islands to prevent further protests.)

Madhu, who was at the forefront of the action says, 'It was a watershed moment for Vimochana in Bangalore. It really brought everyone on the streets. But it was also confusing. The extreme right, the extreme left together with feminists! The discourse in terms of protest was laid down by the right wing. A BJP woman said she would burn herself if the beauty pageant took place in Bangalore. We had to fight for our own space, differentiate our own language and make it clear that we were talking about the global politics of the beauty industry.'

Within days, the matter became serious. Picketing and dharnas escalated to arrests of women protestors and immolation threats. The Bangalore women's groups issued a statement to make their position clear, endorsed by women's groups around the country.

In solidarity, women's groups in other cities mobilized, gathering in rallies, doing street plays on the issue, and distributing pamphlets at busy corners. FAOW led the protests in Bombay. In Delhi, they were organized by Saheli and other groups outside the *Times of India* office, who were the sponsors of the event.[36]

Laxmi Murthy, member of Saheli at the time, recalls the 'huge discussions and introspection amongst us'. She says, 'I remember a poster we made in that period which said "Khane ko nahi roti, Dhoondne chale beauty" [We have no food to eat, But here we are searching for beauty],' which reflected the underlying spirit of the protest: Women's groups were less bothered with 'vulgarity' and more with seeing this as a 'sign of imperialism, a shift in priorities'.

As Laxmi says, 'The winners of beauty pageants suddenly being from Argentina, Venezuela, India was directly linked to increasing market outreach of multinationals selling cosmetics and personal care products. That was what we were protesting. And it did happen.' Mary John wrote in an important piece[37] in the aftermath of the protests, 'Notice also how far the world of advertising has evolved from the earlier degrading if not the crude use of women's bodies for male gratification. As active and vital consumers in their own right, women are both depicted and addressed differently.'

In the long run, women's groups were proved right.

Kalpana says, 'In hindsight, the critique of globalization and the argument about it being a move to exploit India as a market was apt. The market did open up, and in a way we couldn't have imagined. I don't think though we had great impact – it was quite a fringe kind of thing. It was the force of history and the force of economics at the time, and we couldn't keep up.'

—◆—

MS. WORLD BEAUTY PAGEANT: OUR PROTEST
(Statement issued by women's groups, 1996, Bangalore)

'We, the undersigned organisations, working consistently on issues related to violence against women, human rights, poverty etc. over the past 15 years in the city of Bangalore, have been voicing our opposition to the Miss World Contest through peaceful means over the past few months.

For us the protest is not so much about the "vulgar" and "obscene" projection of women, nor definitely a fundamentalist paranoia of "corruption of Indian culture". Our protest is against an event that is a glamorous symbol of the globalisation process that is drawing all Third World and "developing" economies into the highly exploitative international market – in which there is a deepening divide between the rich and the poor, in which the woman and her body is yet another commodity to be bought and sold at a price.

We protest the marketing of a beauty myth that is fragmented, homogenising and standardising the notion of beauty itself – that is being defined and promoted primarily by the cosmetic industry that does not appreciate women's beauty but only seeks to appropriate it for obvious monetary gain.

It is shocking to state that the (Karnataka) government of J.H.Patel, in its attempt to "showcase Bangalore city" to this global market and "have the pageant at all costs" have literally created a curfew-like situation in the city.

However, it is a telling comment that a private cultural event has to be held under total state patronage and such heavy military and police security. It reveals not only the nature of corporate stakes involved in the successful completion of the event but also the extent to which the government is committed to its policy of liberalisation and economic reforms, that will bring nothing but poverty and misery to a majority and prosperity to the few.

In this context, we condemn strongly the unwarranted comments of Police Commissioner S.C.Burman who has exceeded the limits of his office by threatening to clamp down sternly on all protests and protestors who have been dismissed by him as "vulgar riff raff".

Friends and relatives of the 16 girls who were arrested on October 29, 1996 in a protest action were detained, interrogated and arrested as "abettors to a conspiracy". Such expressions of contempt and control by a guardian of law and order flout all the basic norms of a democratic and free society. In the interest of justice we demand that after having been arrested under the law of the land for disturbing the peace, all charges against the women be unconditionally dropped – for their protests were an expression of dissent in a democratic society. This would be also in the spirit of the recent High Court judgment on the issue.

We question also the sincerity of the invitation extended by Amitabh Bachchan, Julia Morley and ABCL, the organisers of the event, on the eve of the pageant for a talk with the protestors for it is nothing but a publicity gimmick to whitewash their own image.

On the other hand, as women's groups that have been protesting various forms of exploitation and violence in society, particularly against women, we also express serious concern about the negative tone of the protests that have drawn groups of different political and ideological orientation – ranging from the extreme Right to the extreme Left.

We are concerned that the nature and form of many of these protests have trivialised the whole issue in the name of culture and sensationalised it by putting forward threats of self-immolation or bombing the venue. We strongly feel that in this issue, violence in our protests whether against the organisers, the event itself or against oneself, is totally unwarranted and can in fact be counterproductive and irresponsible.

We therefore appeal to those women who are threatening to immolate themselves not to throw away their lives. We would urge them instead to stay alive and focus their energies on the more serious issues underlying the pageant – that of consumerism and commodification that is overwhelming women's lives today, leading to an increasing degradation and devaluation of women's true strength and beauty.'

VIMOCHANA * WOMEN'S VOICE * MANINI * MANASA * STREE JAGRUTHI SAMITI

—⟋⟍—

The history of feminism in America is quite inseparable from the history of protests against beauty pageants. It was at the 1969 Miss Atlanta pageant that the protestors outside symbolically tossed many items of clothing into a large dustbin (including perhaps the odd bra) that gave them the 'bra burning' name. It was also at this pageant that the divide was created between women inside the pageant, and those picketing outside.

Fashion had always been separate from politics. But suffragettes in USA had used elements of fashion in their own ways,[38] even being responsible (as Amelia Bloomer was, for publicizing what came to be called the 'bloomer') for innovations in women's clothing. The legend goes that suffragettes wore green, white and violet flowers to symbolize their protest against women not being allowed to vote. (These colours were chosen because their initials GWV for Green, White and Violet also stood for Give Women Votes.) But with the pageant protests, the divide between fashion and feminism became wider, and in later years the two would come to be seen as oil and water.

Even though a faint glimmer of gender-bending sparkled from time to time in fashion (mostly women 'manning it up' in an attempt to symbolize equal competency at the workplace), its propensity to push women to seek ideal bodies or invest self-worth in clothes, bags or shoes made it unpopular with feminists.

Also contributing to fashion's bad name in feminist circles was its precarious position on the edge of porn. Images were overtly sexualized, advertising agencies falling over themselves to be more controversial and eye catching than the next, resulting in a visual vocabulary that contributed to what came to be called in academic circles as 'the sexualization of culture'. A kinder name was 'fashion porn' to distinguish it from mainstream pornography, an issue that had polarized feminists across the continent in what was called the 'sex wars'.

Many of America's most iconic ads were also the most sexist ones. This stoked fires between feminists and the entire advertising machinery (including models who had made important career advances because of these ads) and the faultlines between them cracked wide open to separate them for a long time to come.

In India, the Bangalore protests were the first major signs of such antagonism. Feminist leaders had their own home grown stories to tell about fashion and feminism – like a young Brinda Karat and Madhu Kishwar (both spokespersons for women's rights in later years) sparring in their college, the former having been part of such a contest and the latter virulently opposing it – but after the Bangalore protests, in public memory and to each other, these two sets of women (protestors and the pageantors) became positioned as opposites.

The undercurrent of animosity would mean that feminists would have to keep any delight in fashion and clothes a guilty secret and fashionistas would have to feign disinterest in 'feminist' issues and stop short of making demands for equality, lest they be labelled 'feminist'. They would also, for a long while, stop listening to one another.

—◊◊◊—

Shadows of the Miss World Bangalore protests loomed over the beginning of the millennium. When I started working with a feminist group in 1997, one of my first tasks was to make an info-pack on the media reportage of the protests to be sent out to smaller feminist groups around the country. A poster turned up on my bedroom wall: a cartoon of an impoverished woman with a malnourished child wearing a sash that said 'Miss Starvation'.

Above my desk was a bookmark that said 'Riot Don't Diet' with a silhouette of a fuzzy haired girl in bootcut pants.

Conversations had started, in pockets, on beauty, sexuality and feminist representation of these. Madhu says of the aftermath, 'It was the first time we started looking at "beauty". We had only been firefighting violence against women, but never systematically looked at how women affirmed themselves. Although we'd been organizing film festivals since the 1980s on women and media, after this the attempt was to showcase what could be a feminist view or feminist cinema.'

But this promising start was quickly derailed as other urgent issues swallowed the decade: HIV/AIDS, trafficking in women and its conflation with prostitution, and extreme communal violence with the Gujarat carnage in 2002.

Some developments continued to push feminists to re-examine their positions on women's bodies, labour, sex, and sexuality. A ban on 'bar girls' in Mumbai (women employed to dance in beer bars) in 2005 by the state government of Maharashtra, citing that they were corrupting youth and destroying 'Indian culture', led to 75,000 women losing their livelihoods. Feminist groups in Mumbai got closely involved in defending the women's right to livelihoods.

Meanwhile, a rising and vocal sex workers' rights movement was emerging to fight discrimination and violence against sex workers. This pushed women's groups to reflect on their own position on prostitution. A range of positions was held by different groups in the women's movement including the traditional view, that prostitution was a form of exploitation and women in prostitution need to be rescued and rehabilitated into other less 'immoral activities'. Many groups moved to a more empathetic understanding through listening to sex workers' rights groups: that prostitution could be looked at as a form of informal labour – 'sex work' – and what was important was to look into the conditions of their labour and protect their rights as sex workers.

Thus, in both cases the urge to defend women's rights as workers overshadowed everything else. Jaya notes how the controversial issues were 'neatly settled as labour questions, rights of sex workers – not the right to do sex work'. She reflects, 'We didn't really thrash out why women choose to be in the fashion industry, pornography, even in sex work, because then we would run into more troubled waters. It was easier not to go there.'

This unfinished conversation erupted at an unsuspecting moment during the seventh National Conference of Autonomous Women's Movements in Kolkata in 2006. Attended by about 3,000 women from all over India, the Kolkata conference included for the first time several marginalized groups who participated in large numbers: women with disabilities, sex workers, LGBT activists, and transgender groups including hijras. It also included the dance bar girls from Mumbai and their representatives who were fighting against the state government's ban.

One night, the bar girls were given a platform to dance as part of the cultural programme, open only to women in the conference. Some of them performed to foot-tapping, flirty Bollywood numbers, and exhorted members of the audience to join them in their gyrations. Some of us did, bringing out our sexy moves for the first time at a feminist conference. Then, a leader of the sex workers' movement who was in the audience went up on stage during a dance and gave the girls money in appreciation, all in the spirit of the moment.

The bar girls did not appear to take offence but others in the audience did. They found this degrading to the women dancers, an affirmation of the sexual objectification of women and the exploitation of women's oppression, especially of Dalit women.[39] A large number staged a walkout, disrupting the show.

Discussions afterwards revealed strong opinions on both sides about whether bar dancing amounted to the sexual objectification of women or not. Their performance *had* been strongly sexual in nature (some used the word 'titillation') with their costumes being skimpy ghaghra-cholis. Although such dancing was common on TV and in films, seeing it up close and personal for many had been a first. Discussions ended in a stalemate.

The experience of that night forced many present to rethink their own moral baggage. Perhaps the women's groups had been offended by the challenges this posed to their own deeply held beliefs about sex and sexuality. Sex for pleasure was 'right'. Sex for

money was 'wrong', unless under 'choice-less' circumstances. Sex
for the self was 'right'. Sex for the male gaze was 'wrong'.

Morality had divided everyone, even drawing a line between
the bar dancers and sex workers who one might have thought
of as natural allies, huddled under the umbrella of stigmatized
occupations. Sex workers' groups had been specifically asked by
the bar dancers associations not to vocally support the bar dancers
initiative as they did not want to be associated with the sex workers
groups. The bar dancers, alleged the sex workers, thought of
themselves as being more 'honourable' and having a higher status
than sex workers.[40]

The incident brought to light a fundamental paradox:
supporting the struggle for a livelihood (bar dancing) but seeing
that very livelihood as exploitative. It was difficult for many
to grapple with the choice that bar dancers were apparently
making in wanting to continue in the profession. They could
appreciate (reluctantly) bar dancing as a way of earning a
livelihood in the abstract, but hackles were immediately raised
as the visible exchange of money took place, as if a facade had
been lifted.

—⁓—

By the end of the 2000s the composition of women's groups was
beginning to change. New generations of feminists were joining
these groups, young women who embraced a 'sex-positive'
feminism and had different relationships with their bodies.

Jaya says, 'We got challenged by young people like Rituparna,
and other queer women. When she joined (Delhi-based women's
group) Nirantar 10 years ago, to have her skimpily clad in office
was a new experience, but so wonderful and liberating.'

Although not all older feminists felt that way.

Jaya remembers a women's studies conference at which her
younger colleague wore a sari, with the pallu barely covering her
breasts. 'An older feminist passing by pulled her pallu and covered
the younger woman's shoulders!' She laughs, 'We had some deep
unlearning to do to be able to wear certain clothes. It was certainly

very hard to wear revealing clothes because being a "good woman" or a "good feminist" was very deeply ingrained in us.'

The unspoken norm of being a 'good feminist' was, in previous generations, dressing with a certain austerity that blotted out their elite or middle class backgrounds. Kalpana recalls an incident between a feminist activist leader from the slum community saying to a middle class activist, 'All of you may be wearing khadi kurtas outside but the difference is what you're wearing inside,' referring to the cotton bra slum women would be wearing versus the 1,000 rupee bras the middle class activists wore. It pointed to a sort of hypocrisy amongst middle class feminists.

But it wasn't as if activists of this generation were careless about their appearance. Kalpana says, 'We all wear a certain kind of FabIndia clothes. So it's not true that we don't care about these things at all.'

Jaya says, 'My colleague and I used to love wearing large earrings and ghaghras when we worked in rural Rajasthan. My colleague's husband asked us once, "what kind of feminists are you going around wearing big earrings?" It was interesting he saw a contradiction there. How far we've come from that! Can't imagine having a conversation like that today!'

Jaya remembers when a well-known activist came to speak at a women's studies conference in the mid 80s wearing lipstick, and 'everybody was all nudge-nudge wink-wink, as if it was most outrageous'.

With the new generation, concerns like lipstick were no longer an issue. Young women now wanted to present themselves as sensual and sexy, as a backlash to repression and being told to be modest.

Rishita Nandagiri, sexual health and rights activist, says, 'For some of us, lipstick is a sign of defiance. If you put on red lipstick, what does it say about you?' Now worn with pride, red lipstick was a sign of resistance, of challenging 'slut-shaming'. This generation was invested specially in rejecting the sexual politics of shame and honour, reclaiming public spaces, taking back the night, and presenting a sassy challenge to existing sexual moralities. Questions of desire, pleasure, autonomy were attractive to this newer generation of feminists, who often spoke within a framework of 'choice'.

But choice, for previous generations, had been a complex and difficult terrain. They had burnt their fingers trying to understand women's 'agency' – or why women would wilfully and knowingly choose to do acts that were harmful to the feminist agenda. Such as choosing to have sex selective abortions, or choosing to follow unequal rituals like karvachauth (the fast women in northern India kept for their husbands' longevity). Or women choosing to join right wing groups and political parties.

—ᴍ—

Concerns around objectification and commodification receded like a wave, as the new decade – the 2010s – was fraught with the rise of right wing politics.

Under the onslaught of right wing articulations in the public arena, women's groups came out in defense of everything the right wing targeted as 'trespassing of Indian culture'. From the abuse and trolling of 'item girls' (women performing a crowd-pulling sexy song number in Bollywood films) to attacks on girls out at night or in pubs, to diktats against girls wearing jeans, to censorship of all kinds. They struggled against the many conservative tentacles that began to close in on the gains they had made over the decades.

The demonization of Islam also made discussion on objectification of women politically volatile. Any discussion of the bikini would immediately draw up parallels with the demonization of women in hijab. 'We wanted to distance ourselves from right wing moralism,' says Mary John.

The conversation on objectification and commodification remained deferred, as women's groups mobilized to hold their ground in a hostile and dangerous political and economic climate. Mary says, 'We have retreated from a bare attack on objectification but are still finding our feet when it comes to the larger picture. There are fewer jobs available for women that do *not* involve objectification except maybe domestic work and primary school teaching. There is an overall glamourising taking place of workplaces, flight attendants, even BPO workers who glamourize their voices. What is neoliberalism doing to our economy? It's a small part of the larger question we are worried about.'

—ᴟᴟ—

Most of the younger generation of feminists hadn't heard of the Miss World Bangalore protests. The new generation saw little contradiction in their version of feminism, and fashion. Market feminism was pushing both newer and older feminists to engage with fashion in new ways, through the medium of great conversation of our time: the internet.

An interesting new genre of blogging was now also visible, that of feminist fashion blogging. Japleen Pasricha, founder of the website Feminism in India (started as a Facebook page in 2013 after the uprising against sexual assault that followed the 'Nirbhaya' case), says, 'We decided to have a feminist fashion blogger to have articles on body positivity. The focus is on dealing with body image issues, not to cover fashion.'

This generation is frank about growing up with body image issues. 'Adolescence was not kind to me,' says Amba Salelkar wryly. Amba is a former criminal lawyer and now disability rights activist. 'Fat, braces, being bullied. As a 14 year old growing up in Goa I would feel like a misfit among girls in my class. Those were awkward times – growing up as a gawky teenager as Miss Worlds were redefining beauty in India.'

Japleen says, 'My mum is very fair. I'm not. I have a regular wheatish complexion. As a child I used to get lot of comments on it, as for Punjabis [fairness] is so valued in the community. I internalized the belief that I was the "ugly duckling" as I would see it come up on a daily basis at home.'

Engaging with fashion was part and parcel of their coming of age, their coming to terms with its inherent biases without rejecting it altogether. Amba remembers, 'We used to buy these copies of Cosmopolitan for 10 bucks on Bombay trains. They would have fashion tips depending on your body type. For instance – don't cut your hair short if you have a round face. So I didn't dare try cutting my hair for a long time. I did later when I moved to Chennai and it looked great! And I was like, people of whatever face shape should cut their hair short if they want to! It looks good on everyone! The fashion tips were more like dogmas – "don't wear stripes on stripes". We can wear stripes on stripes! It's cool!'

Amba feels the internet has changed the game by creating a platform for multiple voices on everything, including fashion. She says, 'I really like fashion bloggers and vloggers (video bloggers) – people who are of various races, shapes, abilities, income levels, and are united in wanting to look good and presentable, and even fashionable. We want to look good – but it can't be a pressure brought about by an industry. We *need* different people authoring the glamour discourse.'

Amena Azeez is a plus size fashion blogger and body positive advocate, and guest writer at Feminism in India. Amena's blog, Fashionopolis, (which now sees 20,000 to 30,000 people visiting it every month) focuses on plus size fashion, body positivity and fat activism, born of her own experience of years of body shaming and body image issues. She says, 'I've stopped reading fashion magazines. They gave me massive body issues as a teenager. Nothing promotes self hate as these magazines.' When Amena started to read international blogs by plus size fashion bloggers, she says it was an 'eye opener, a revelation to me', so conditioned was she to this think 'nothing will look good on me'. All the don't-do-this and don't-do-that of fashion magazines – 'no crop tops, no horizontal stripes, no sheer clothes' – split at the seams. 'You can wear it all!' she exulted.

Amena has a bone to pick with feminists though. 'Feminists in India are hardly doing anything on body positivity and fat acceptance. Are you seeing any Indian feminist zines visibly putting fat size women celebrating themselves? It is only lip service. There will be multiple articles on abortion laws in the USA but barely anything on body positivity in India.'

Rishita also follows several edgy fashion blogs that she feels are 'browning and queering' the discourse. 'There's a fashion brand that had trans women model their saris. That was interesting,' she says, although she worries this is 'exoticization' that's using political ideas to sell products. 'I don't know if it's moving anything forward, but it is opening up conversations.' She speaks of a Nike ad she saw recently which shows all kinds of women, running. 'It's Nike, so it's ridiculously expensive. But the important idea is that you need a space, to run. Which we don't have. It's no longer about being skinny but being fit,' she says. 'Although the women still look the same way.'

For Amba, the liberating aspect of the internet has been e-commerce, and the way it enables disabled and trans persons to access all kinds of clothes and looks. She says, 'People in the process of transitioning aren't comfortable shopping for lingerie and the like. Women with disabilities find the changing room atmosphere inaccessible. It's hard to get into a changing room, there are questions, staring, privacy issues. Now being able to do this in the privacy of your home has really made lots of people more comfortable.'

There is a refreshing frankness in the ether about the pleasures of ornamentation and dressing up – for the self. Not just for the younger generation. Older generations of feminists are on their own journeys of experimentation. Jaya says, 'I was 47 and I'd never worn high heels. When I came into the BDSM[41] community though, wearing those high heels made so much sense as a form of sexual expression; OTT, sexy, playful, a performance. All those things one couldn't access as a feminist, maybe? I cursed my feminism because of which I had never worn high heels! I found it very liberating when I went to a party and exchanged my extremely high heels with a queer male bodied person, who wanted to wear them as an expression of queerness. It was an act of aesthetic solidarity.'

Kalpana says of her own self, 'I have personally found that I do like to dress up. Wear lipstick. I do colour my hair. I don't want to put on weight, all that stuff. I am conscious of myself, within a certain aesthetic.' Mary jokes about cutting her hair short after having had long hair for 50 years. She says, 'People say I look good. I believe them 30 per cent.'

The internet has brought multiple voices into the ring. Every day is a renewed conversation on gender, discrimination, sexism, violence and proudly and loudly – on feminism itself.

Feminism has become fashionable, to the surprise of older generations of feminists, and attracts many likes and shares on social media. But many in the younger generation are critical of this, especially when it's used as currency in advertising. Japleen even has a term for it. 'Femvertising is a huge thing,' she says. 'Feminism is the new sellout and every brand is using it. At the end of the day, they want to sell products.'

But it is constantly forcing different generations of feminist activists to re-engage with fashion, the body, and sexuality.

Laxmi says, 'I saw this feature online in which a fashion photographer used the maid in her office as a model. The girl had that typical Western model look – tall, thin, wide shoulder, thin waist. You couldn't tell she hadn't done it before.' The piece made Laxmi question her own assumptions. 'You assume they're part of the glamour world, their outward appearance with the pout, the sultry look and the drape of clothes. It looks like they've spent years and years of perfecting it. But when you know that it is a domestic help, someone who does jhadu pocha who is the model, it breaks down that assumption. It made me think of how photographs establish a reality. Despite the intelligence or information we have, we often can't believe it when things are not as they seem in an image.'

It is this image the internet has shaken up, by allowing those inside the images to break through and represent themselves as living, thinking beings. It has opened up an unusual space to talk about how someone can choose to be apparently 'objectified' but still be a feminist icon – two things that were once hard to reconcile. Sunny Leone, a former porn industry star, becomes a feminist icon because of the way she resists being put down and shamed in an interview for her life choices. Qandeel Baloch, Pakistani model and internet darling because of her racy pictures and unapologetic sass, becomes a feminist icon when she is tragically shot by her own brother to avenge the 'dishonour' she has brought to their family.

Japleen says, 'Qandeel Baloch doesn't have a Masters in women's studies or work in a women's group, but her quote on speaking up is really good. Even if she posted pics of her body, her posts are really inspirational. So how do we define who is a feminist? She was a model posting half-nude pics but her words next to the pic were very empowering.'

Things that seemed simpler in the past, more black and white, appeared now in their many shades of grey. Thinking back to the Miss World Bangalore protests, Laxmi says, 'The trauma created by such contests for young girls, in terms of the pressure for a certain body image – that critique is valid. But we were stuck in that without thinking of what the women and girls in (the pageant) were thinking. It was all "down down", "ban", "don't commodify", "women are not your playthings", "selling of women's bodies". We never thought we should engage with the women themselves.'

Madhu also reflects on this, 'The women's movement also, in a way, objectified women participating in the pageants. Saw them as victims. Didn't see them as women with an opinion. It was a big flaw. Today we would say let's talk to the woman first.'

The resistance to beauty pageants proved futile for a number of reasons, according to Laxmi. The lack of a visible enemy, the proliferation of pageants in every locality that made protest unviable, and most conspicuously, no 'victims'. She says, 'What you think is exploitative might not align with the view of the people you are fighting on behalf of. This is most difficult for feminists to accept. It's much easier when there is a victim or someone on whose behalf you are taking up cudgels. Someone you can show as having been harmed. But here there are no ready victims. Many of those participating in it are ok – they will say buzz off we are fine. That's where protests hit a roadblock,' says Laxmi.

Is that why feminists don't protest beauty pageants any more? 'Feminists also don't protest dowry deaths any more,' says Laxmi. 'In the 1980s we protested outside every clinic doing sex determination tests! But not anymore. There's been a very high level of burnout. At another level we need to rethink some things.'

Younger generations of feminists are not fully on board with beauty pageants either, even though many dis-enfranchised communities – trans women, persons with disabilities, acid attack victims – celebrate their bodies and their difference through such pageants. Amba acknowledges that 'Things like the Miss Wheelchair pageant – it does make some participants very happy to be part of it'. However she has mixed feelings about it. She says, 'I'm wary that it creates pressures on others by prioritizing women with disabilities who embody a certain conventional beauty. This might be creating a hierarchy of women with disabilities – favouring women who don't have impairments that mar their facial features. The media tries to coopt women with disabilities into ad campaigns with slogans like "you're beautiful inside" or you have a "beautiful heart". I can understand that this can be validation for many, but as a feminist I feel conflicted about it.'

Rishita adds, 'Beauty pageants inherently value the wrong things. They valorize beauty. It's still about your body. That shouldn't be the point, to be up for comparison and to be judged against some arbitrary criteria.'

For Amba though, calling for a ban on them is out of the question. She says, 'It's a mode of expression, for what it's worth. Can't ban freedom of expression.'

Japleen says, 'I'm not sure I'd like to protest beauty pageants, not that I think it's great. The point is for young women to understand that showing or not showing their body is their decision – an informed choice. It is complicated in my mind at the moment.' She relates it to the banning of hijabs in France. 'Either we tell women to show or cover (their body). Both are not ok. I wouldn't want to tell someone to enter (or not enter) a beauty pageant or wear or remove the hijab. It's not for me to speak.'

Between freedom of expression and choice: between a rock and a hard place. This is where conversations have often stumbled. As Amba says, 'This is the conflict within feminism. When someone says something is their "choice" people tend to back off. What one needs is a healthy questioning of these choices to unpack them.'

Laxmi reflects, 'I wouldn't protest beauty pageants now. But I'd probably do the same thing if I went back in time. What I'd do differently is I'd try to listen more to the people participating.'

At the heart of the matter though, the question – of how to look at women's individual choices that undermine or do not further the advancement of womankind – remains. Jaya says, 'There is something very incomplete about the conversation on agency in the women's movement. We don't even have the words.' Mary says of the current moment, 'Now we have pretty young men in ads. There are more ads of men in underwear than there are of women. Today we have Sunny Leone (a Canadian porn star now working in Bollywood), but feminists have not taken positions on this.'

Laxmi says, 'Looking back, there was quite a level of squeamish discomfort with women being on stage semi-clad, being pretty casual about it. There was a discomfort and continues to be. But we are now couched in politically correct language and feminists have not addressed this fully.'

For Madhu and many other activists the burning issue is not beauty pageants or objectification and commodification anymore but the everyday battle against persistent sexism, discrimination and violence. Fashion and feminism are, for the moment, allies.

Madhu says, 'Whether you're fashion models or whatever, feminism is more diffused now – not necessarily in the way we'd wanted – but they're also challenging patriarchy wherever they are. Finally that's what one can hope for.'

LAST WORDS

Ladies with an attitude
Fellas that were in the mood
Don't just stand there
Let's get to it
Strike a pose
There's nothing to it

Madonna, 'Vogue' 1990.

Chapter twelve

Not Just a Mannequin

As glamour was being packaged and sold to Indian women by ingenious magazine editors and feminist groups were protesting the 'integration of India into a highly exploitative international market', something important was happening unnoticed.

A new class of working women was being formed.

Girls were coming from across social classes, plotting to be part of this new workforce that seemed to offer a shot at something big. They were scouring satellite TV, poring over glossies, to learn how to read the signposts to this highway of social mobility, sending off awkward photos of themselves in shiny jackets and pants in neighbourhood photo studios to beauty pageant organizers. They were readying to plunge into this exciting new winning field where there seemed to be no English-speaking, passport-demanding guards at the gate preventing entry. And where women seemed to be on top.

They were disappointed, of course. What seemed like a global, modern profession (which it was, in terms of the time period and context in which it came into prominence in the West) based on merit and impersonal, professional relationships turned out to be not free of conservatism. It was strongly influenced by existing Indian models of patronage and networks of personal alliances where transactions were made usually on the basis of friendships amongst class peers. A seniority-based hierarchy existed behind the scenes rather than egalitarian relations or a system of ascendancy based on merit.

A Sudanese woman from a war-torn village or a Vietnamese woman from a poverty-torn one could go from rags to riches in this field (as the international fashion world had seen),[42] but an Indian girl from a village or even a small town met subtle rules of inclusion and exclusion. An inherent bias seemed to prevail that privileged English, cultural capital, urban sensibilities, sophistication, and a minimal level of human development with regard to nutrition, education and infrastructure, and knowledge of 'trade secrets' – ways of disciplining the body, trickeries of maquillage, dieting footnotes and rules of self-presentation.

Neither was it really a women-dominated industry. Merely because it comprised a disproportionate number of women as compared to men because of the gendered demands of fashion, advertising and marketing, it didn't translate into better status for women. In the larger hierarchy of the glamour industry, most models were seen as mute mannequins or designers' muses, with little creative potential of their own. 'We don't have a voice. That is known from the beginning. We are there to be looked at,' Vinita had said to me grimly.

You would think the economies of glamour would be organized, structured with well-built systems, but a closer look showed in it characteristics of the informal sector – unskilled, with a floating labour population, relative ease of entry, operating on informal transactions, with no minimum remuneration, a chain of third parties facilitating work between two parties and the absence of any institutionalized body to oversee or regulate matters arising from conflict. Parts of the industry – the agencies to some extent – showed some semblance of structure but often operated in opaque ways.

One thing though, was true.

It did offer social mobility in the new India that had not been possible for women before. Those who met some of its minimal qualifications, even with shaky pedigree, could climb its rungs with a plan, with luck, by aligning with an international agency, and in some cases, by simply not giving up.

Being a model with some success and visibility meant a shot at stepping across class and caste boundaries. It meant that Pragati from working class East Delhi and Tina from posh South Delhi, from two vastly different ends of the social spectrum, could share the same platform at their agency and have equal chances at something. (Ironically, Pragati has modelled for international magazines while Tina has done shoots for Indian language women's magazines.)

The girls were pushed to 'grow up quick', to transform from ugly ducklings to graceful swans, to perform not just gender but enact class and embody globalization. A model's lifestyle after all, often exemplifies it – endless travel, moving not just from city to city for shows but transitioning between compartments of the traditional and the modern in trips back to conservative hometowns, in a whirl of images, and in the eternal service of global capital. She embodies with her miraculous transformation how a nation too can transform. Get a 'make-over'.

Like Pragati or Shivani or Kavita can emerge swan-like with their newfound global knowledge, so can India.

But the darker side was also true. It only applied to some kinds of people. What is the formula that puts some kinds of people on the upside of globalized India, and pushes others further and further into exclusion, rightlessness, invisibility?

Like Mayuri, a school drop out from a village in Assam.

While girls like Pragati (from a Hindi medium school in East Delhi), Kavita (convent educated from Agra) and Shivani (from a conservative household in Benaras) manage to create a niche in the industry, Mayuri's obstacles were still too prohibitive. Besides the disadvantage of cultural and class distance, she was subject to another kind of viciousness in the industry: intolerance for those who are more than ordinarily disadvantaged with regard to English, modernity and urbanity. Mayuri had caught onto this rejection, and therefore, hoped to bypass this class system, by aiming instead (like others before her) for the international modelling scenario – where those very qualities that brought condescension and derisive smirks in India (accent, being from a village, her 'tribal' looks), would be applauded as exotic.

Who wins and who loses in this new India? Who decides?

—ༀ—

The struggle to convince society that many of the things women do have economic meaning has been a long one. And even when they have been acknowledged as having some economic value (by becoming paid labour from unpaid), the social value is still missing. The status accorded to some types of work isn't always linked to money but on what that work actually is.

Household work, caring for the young and the old, and other forms of invisible work that women do is usually given a lower status. Even when there is a payment involved for domestic work, sex work or childcare, they remain low in status, historically having struggled to be counted as 'real work'. Modelling is part of this basket of controversial economic goods.

You put on some fancy clothes and make up, walk down a ramp – sashay is the word that underlines the effortlessness of it all – change and repeat. What's there? There's quite a lot actually. Hidden behind the popular perception of their 'non-work' is the actual labour that goes into producing fashion images or advertisements. Because we don't identify modelling with labour, we don't understand it when models organize for their rights, or when there are calls for fair labour standards. That some problems exist is evident from efforts by previous generations of models to organize for their rights in the form of a union.

But the inability to imagine any other form of collective other than a union or think only in terms of the straitjacketed protection offered by the agency (to profitable and loyal subjects) is a symptom of a larger malaise. Most middle class working women don't know how to associate with each other to articulate their needs for a better working environment or ways to enhance their productivity. Where do you go to express an opinion, dissent or needs beyond stationery? At most, you go to HR.

Even though there are all sorts of precedents in India where women have organized into collectives to make their voices heard and demands counted, perhaps it is too much to expect middle class women to embrace these learnings from women workers of other socio economic realities. Will they, could they, ever acknowledge that they need new ways of organizing? That there are things to learn from struggles of self-help groups, sex workers or fisherwomen? That they may need 'workers' rights'? The women I interviewed were often stumped when asked what kinds of rights as workers models should get.

Some of the strains from the narratives have larger ramifications about work in globalizing India. For example, the idea that 'Indian' labour is usually cheap – at whatever level and whatever form of work – in the way an international agency views Indian models vis a vis foreign models doing the same work.

Modelling involves participating in a creative but segmented and stratified industry, where there are all kinds of working conditions and situations. Where a vulnerability to certain kinds of abuse exists, but no remedial measures for it have been even thought about, forget being institutionalised. Models are clearly not 'victims'. They chart their career paths, make decisions about what kinds of work to do or not, network to generate work for themselves from the market. Anupriya told me with a wry smile, 'We do have our own senses, you know. We are not just mannequins that someone can do whatever on us they want to do.'

But the perception is just that! The industry does not entirely see them as full human beings. And beyond all their other challenging experiences, this is the one that cuts deepest.

Inanimate objects are indiscriminately used to describe what models are supposed to be: 'just puppets', 'mannequin', 'clothes hanger', 'muse'. Soon, women begin to believe that while tailors, designers and fitters tuck, drape and pin garments onto their still bodies, they are not supposed to move or complain or disturb this activity, even if a pin pricks them. Their body or feelings are secondary to the task at hand.

In themselves, they are nothing – they need a network of designers, make-up artists, photographers, clients to become a 'model'. They are a form to be 'worked on', whether by the make-up artist or the designer or stylist. They are the canvas on which an artist expresses himself. This constant analogy can contribute to making them seem less human, in the eyes of those around them, and give the women themselves a diminished sense of social value.

Alongside, they are fed other myths: what really distinguishes a good model from a bad one is 'attitude' or 'personality' – a quality with a strong sense of personhood. An inanimate object – a puppet, a mannequin or a hanger – cannot have 'attitude'. The 'x factor' or 'star value' that dictates the random amount a successful model can command in the market is also linked to her innate personality. Which is it, then, a confused model will ask? Do I have to be a mute mannequin or be a sparkling personality? How can I be both?

Dogged by these contradictory perceptions, only a partial personhood is 'allowed' to women in the industry. She is a persona non grata, 'an unwelcome person', allowed occasionally to express that part of her personality that is marketable or in line with the overall gains of the client or industry. It is ironical that women who appear to be at the centre of the glamour economy, and living carriers or advertisements of all that the glamour economy has to offer, are often marginal, voiceless and rarely the ones 'calling the shots'.

—w—

Imagine a stream. At one end of the stream stands a nun. She stands for asexual work: where the element of sexuality is conspicuously absent. At the other end of the stream let us have the others – those in whose occupation the element of sexuality is fully present. Sex workers. Women in prostitution. 'Ladies of the night'.

Imagine along the stream we position women whose work involves body work or sexuality with varying degrees. Somewhere in the middle may be a nurse. A little further towards the end could be bar dancers, strippers, nautanki or laavani dancers. Item girls. Perhaps some models – the toothpaste models finding place much before the swimsuit calendar ones.[43]

Now imagine a thermometer that measures stigma, let's call it a stigmometer.

Dip it into the nun side of the stream and it does nothing, as cold as a corpse. Take it further up, and a light starts to flicker. Ah, here there are women who travel a lot and are therefore under social suspicion (corporate ladies?), ladies who come home late at night and therefore under social suspicion (media women?),

women who are known to smoke and drink (feminist activists?), women who have too many male colleagues or friends (investment bankers?) – other factors temper the waters and the stigmometer is quick to react. It turns yellow at the Bollywood starlets, then orange at the models and by the time you've reached the sex workers it's blinking a flaming red.

The correlation between sexuality, labour and stigma is what we see on this continuum. The more chaste you appear, the less stigma you will face.

People think of female sexuality in different ways. One way of seeing it, as religious texts or local patriarchies do, is as an uncontrolled, dangerous, threatening, polluting animal, culturally the source of personal and community shame and honour. In this version female sexuality must be contained and controlled, come what may. This is the formulation feminists have been struggling against for years, battling its implications: that once she become an adolescent she must practice 'modesty' that traps her in the home, that rape is shameful for the woman, that she must be 'preserved' till she marries, that she must marry only someone sanctioned by the community, that she not touch anything while menstruating, that she remember repeatedly that her body is not hers but the family's, the community's, the nation's.

These ideas control women's lives. They curtail our freedom and terrorize us. Women manage their sexualities at the workplace without even knowing it sometimes: dressing according to overt and covert rules ('no sleeveless' in some corporate offices, no cleavage in others), behaving according to good-girl-protocols as per the local context, swallowing sexist talk at lunch breaks or going the other way and 'working it' like many others have before them.

All working women have a place in this stream, and depending on how hard the wind blows, anyone can be swept downstream. This stigma attaches itself to the skin of those in that part of the stream with the fastidiousness of synthetic dyes.

Stigma cannot be easily scrubbed away. Neither can it be surgically removed. Instead it must be managed through a series of clever time-tested ploys: having a stage name (Erving Goffman, the stigma theorist once said 'the average chorus girl changes her name as frequently as her coiffure'), constructing sympathetic biographies, hiding what they do from strangers and the landlord, having a disclosure etiquette ('I model sometimes' or 'I model for friends'), maintaining a physical distance from neighbours, relatives and hometowns, marrying smart, using 'dis-identifiers' that help break the stereotype (wearing glasses, 'I come from a family of doctors', 'I love reading', 'I wear a salwar kameez and no make up otherwise'), and when all else fails, shutting themselves out, wearing dark glasses all the time.

I think often of what the 27 year-old Ruhi described to me. Ruhi lived in the satellite town of Ghaziabad and had been modelling for about six years. To come to Delhi for her meetings and auditions, she would travel to Delhi in the local bus. She needed to be fully covered and as inconspicuous as possible, as a way of avoiding stares or harassment so she would wear an extra jacket or shirt over her audition outfit, and have a scarf to cover her face up so the make up was hidden. If she got harassed in the bus, she said, she would get off and take an auto to another bus stop, and take another bus from there. But there were other problems too: 'The problem is that if you're standing in a bus stand for a long time, people start noticing you....' So Ruhi would take another auto to another bus stop, to avoid this. This was hard, given she was usually carrying a big poly-bag containing her work profile, heels, shirt, jacket and so on.

As she reached her audition venue, she would ask 'if there is a loo somewhere' and go into the toilet to comb her hair, put on makeup, take off the multiple coverings and wipe clean the evidence of the journey: the dirt on her face, the sweat, the wind battered hair. And be ready to be the cynosure of all eyes.

How much longer can we live like Ruhi, between 'spectacle and surveillance'? Like so many other young women in India, she stands between being a spectacle for the media, clients and potential clients where she is encouraged to present herself as a subject of desire, but under surveillance by the general public, even family, relatives, community which is ready to punish her for the same.

When can we stop being different people in different places to avoid stigma and its devastating impacts?

—⁓—

In the end, one question at the heart of my research remained.

Are women in the glamour industry, like the illusion created by the Sushmita Sens and the Aishwarya Rais, empowered? Is it really about 'women's empowerment' as the Managing Director of the Miss India pageant in the television debate insisted? Even after all these pages this is a difficult question to answer. To quote economist Amartya Sen 'Given the many faces of gender inequality, much would depend on which face we look at.'

We've seen that the glamour industry gives women models a lower status, and Indian society, with its double standards doesn't hold them in very good stead. They often have a troubled personal life because of this. Despite this, most of the women I interviewed were economically independent, socially visible, role models for many young women, enjoying material comforts, travelling the world, supporting their families or occasionally their own lifestyles, with many of them living their own lives as they chose and, challenging many traditional norms.

But the stigma associated with their occupation (displaying the self, body parts or posing sensually) charged their personal relationships with a damaging current. At the same time, many also unlearnt years of socialized shame about their body, learning to look at it, care for it and display it objectively. Sometimes, this sexual subjectivity over the years turned into a tendency to make independent sexual choices in their personal lives. Yet the stigma that won't rub off led many to have an ambiguous relationship with their occupation: proud of it and ashamed of it at the same time.

Female desire or a feminist understanding doesn't find place in advertising or fashion as such, and the glamour industry largely confines itself to the enactment of female sexuality for male desire at the macro level (or enactment of class for female consumers). But at the micro level it still involves engagement with self and sexuality that challenges patriarchy and offers women the potential to discover sexual autonomy, dismantle patriarchal shame and experience sexuality as a site for some sort of liberation from traditional strictures and roles.

Empowerment means many things, from the dry language of policy to the visible evidence of resources or independent living. There are umpteen items in this laundry list: economic independence, quality of life, sense of self-worth, security, autonomy in decision making, opportunities for skill building and so on. What isn't on this list though, and never has been, is something more visceral and less tangible. Something that renders the empowerment of even the most empowered, incomplete. That missing element is respectability.

Being perceived and judged as immoral, hypersexual, deviant, public, available and the like leaves most models with a deep sense of what can be described as 'hurt'. Recent feminist literature has started recognizing that like pain (a powerful concept to understand the unsaid in women's lived experiences), hurt too has a role to play in keeping women away from living fulfilled lives. 'Hurt' is beyond just a sense of sadness, it can be a violation of the spirit, 'an everyday unspoken and yet nonetheless frequent experience… an aspect of resistance and constraint in women's lives'.[44]

Even after everything is said and done, a void remains. This void is the absence of respectability, played out with words and gestures, the slut-shaming that shuts women up and locks up their key to being free. Women don't want to subscribe to the old patriarchal notions of shame, honour or respect, but there is a longing, a searing anger, a deep deep well of desire to be respectable, to enjoy a sense of dignity and self-worth that is not challenged by strangers or suspected by lovers.

Even after every other battle is won, this one continues to limit our lives.

Postscript
'We Should All Be Feminists'

Who were we and who are we now?

In 2004 when I started this research, the Indian Congress Party had won a surprise victory in the national elections and a liberal economist – one of the architects of India's globalization dream – Dr Manmohan Singh was sworn in as the Prime Minister of India, for what was to be a decade of Congress rule.

In 2004, a massive tsunami wave arising from an earthquake in the Indian Ocean measuring 9.3 on the Richter scale swept almost 290,000 people into its fold on Christmas day. In 2004, the first iPhone was still in the making. Facebook had just been launched as a private social networking site for students at Harvard University. The final episode of American sitcom *Friends* had aired.

2004 seems very far away now. It is hard to imagine a world without Facebook, iPhones, or reruns of *Friends*.

It is, as they say, 'history'.

It is 2015 and I am on my way to a Fashion Week after 10 years. I am no longer wearing unbranded and inconspicuous jeans and a white shirt that I once thought was classy dressing. No, this time I am in an Anita Dongre russet-coloured kurta with an excellent drape and onion pink (cerise, as they say now) habutai silk harem pants that I bought online from Jaypore. Of course I wear open toed casual sandals, because this is Mumbai. Although it is a different hotel and city, the chaos is as I remember it. The

St. Regis Hotel, Mumbai is hosting Mumbai Fashion Week this spring – one of the many fashion weeks over the year that it will host. I am to pick up my personal invitation from a designated helper but in the chaos the person in possession of the card and I miss each other. Luckily I bump into my friend who is the designer whose show I am invited to, and along with his posse of friends, I am herded into the show area. We take our seats in the Front Row.

It is divine coincidence that on my left sits the former editor of the fashion magazine I had interviewed at LIFW a decade ago. She looks pretty much the same as she did then. She recognizes me. We chat pleasantly. Across from me, in the second row on the other side of the ramp, sits the former beauty editor of another fashion magazine. We have common friends, and I follow her blog. I go across and we greet each other warmly. I'm beginning to feel at home here.

The show is beautiful, the models striking, the clothes careful and elaborate at the same time. I recognize three of the models as my 'interviewees' from my research of 10 years ago. They look the same too.

I don't look the same though.

My body has borne two children since. My hair has obviously greyed. I have moved from a size S to an M over my 40th birthday. I wear Prada spectacles. And today I have worn my guilty-pleasure Chanel earrings – two interlocked crystal Cs with a fake pearl drop. In case anyone should notice.

I am almost fashionable. And still a feminist.

In fact everywhere I see, I see fashionable persons who are also feminists. India is at a moment in time when feminist thoughts are very much mainstream. Incredible changes have taken place this decade: gender equality is part of public conversations; slut shaming is questioned; victim blaming, sexual assault and rape are part of public conversations; cases of sexual harassment at the workplace are coming out into the public domain; questions of body image are commonly discussed; young women and men are out on the streets not afraid to challenge authority, including a regime of intolerance.

Yet at the same time: we are still where we were.

All indices of patriarchy are flying high. The way we look has become more and more important. India has the fourth highest number of cosmetic surgeries in the world – after USA, Brazil and South Korea. India has over 2,000 cosmetic surgeons, comparable to Japan. Young girls – as young as my daughter who is now 11 – struggle with issues of body image. Hundreds of small beauty pageants that continue to proliferate across the country. Millions of young people's dreams still hang on these.

Earlier, in March 2015, social media went into a tizzy over a video made by *Vogue* India called 'My Choice' in which a Bollywood actor, Deepika Padukone, speaks on empowerment and the various things that are 'her choice'.[45] The video drew a varied response: some applause, some anxiety, a few clever parodies. It also drew sharp commentary from socialists to socialites for being 'upper class' and like a 'shampoo ad'. '*Vogue* and Empowerment?' asked some, implying: it's a fashion magazine, what did you expect?

But in reality, fashion and feminism are no longer as distant as they once were. No longer are there protests at beauty pageants. Fashion magazines carry feminist stories routinely: how to handle sexual abuse, reclaim public spaces, address sexual harassment at the workplace, the power of female friendships.

The cover of *Vogue* India for March 2017 has Bollywood actor Anushka Sharma on the cover in a white T-shirt by French luxury conglomerate Dior that's all the rage this season. It says, 'We should all be feminists', taken from a speech that went viral by Nigerian born author Chimananda Ngozi Adichie. The T-shirt costs $710 on Saks Fifth Avenue's website, a part of the proceeds going to a charitable foundation supported by Dior and pop star Rihanna. I don't quite know what to make of it. Should I see it as a victory for the movement or the ultimate commodification of feminism? Does writing a slogan on a T-shirt really challenge anything about patriarchy?

I don't look the same. And I don't feel the same either.

Which makes me wonder: who were we and who are we now?

The once secular, easygoing India to the deeply communal, violent one. The once liberal, family members with barely a passing interest in religion, to actively reclaiming a Hindu identity. A nonjudgmental diversity in food habits to a ban on beef. A constitutional commitment to free speech to a practice of censorship and surveillance. Not all is bad though. Just look at how feminist ideas have captured the imagination of millions of young women across the country.

What changes us? As nations, as a people, as individuals? As a world?

Who were you and who have you become?

The gold rush in glamour has passed. A steady trickle of women (and increasingly men) still make their way to its gates, but other new winning fields have emerged: reality shows, singing contests, dancing competitions, serials, all on TV. Models have slowly been replaced in many TV ads and billboards by film stars and sportspeople, who have discovered how lucrative their brand value in modelling can be, and are now managed by professionals who strike multi-crore rupee deals for them. Even *Vogue* magazine that launched in India in 2007 has preferred to have Bollywood beauties on its cover rather than real fashion models. With other spaces being squeezed for them, most have retreated gracefully to the faithful ramp and the fashion editorials.

A decade has passed since I interviewed 30 women working as models in Delhi and Mumbai. In these years, I've seen how some of them have moved on. Some I met again, in the most unusual places. One (Josy) turned up as a temp teacher in my then one-year-old's playschool. She was trying it out because she had ambitions to start a school of her own someday. I bumped into another (Noelle) outside a pub in London. One became the face of India's best known cosmetics brand. One (Shivani) gladdened my heart when I read she had married for love, and continued working after marriage. In 2005 she could not imagine going against her parents' wish and have a 'love marriage'. One became a DJ. One opened a restaurant with her savings as the sun set on her modeling years. Another (Pragati) continued her ruling the ramp ambition and became visible at every single ramp show. Two debuted in films, one in a prominent film made by one of India's finest directors. One, the one who had opened the doors for my fieldwork, took her own life, hanging herself in her flat in Mumbai.

Of the remaining, a few continue to be where they were – walking the runway, appearing in some ads, moving from Fashion Week to Fashion Week, managing to stay on track.

I remember them all and I wish them well.

Whatever we engage with, changes us. I didn't change them, but I think they changed me.

Notes

1. Tzvetan Todorov. 2008. *Duties and Delights: The Life of a Go-Between: Interviews with Catherine Portevin*. Kolkata: Seagull Books, p. 341.

2. Stephen Gundle. 2008. *Glamour: A History*. New York: Oxford University Press, pp. 2-9.

3. 'When India "Missed" the Universe' by Madhu Kishwar, in *Manushi* no. 88 (1995).

4. 'Ford models to kick off India model hunt' by exchange4media News Service (June 9, 2004). Online at: http://www.exchange4media. com/others/ford-models-to-kick-off-india-model-hunt_12280. html

5. 'Quest for beauty' by a staff writer, *India Today*. (December 31, 1994). Online at: http://indiatoday.intoday.in/story/aishwarya-rai-too-tiny-for-fords-supermodel-contest-says-dominique-caffin/1/294788.html

6. 'Anatomy Lesson', by a staff writer, *Indian Express* (*The Sunday Express Eye*, 18 September 2005). Online at: http://archive.indianexpress. com/oldStory/78257/

7. 'Indian Fashion Industry at a Glance' by a staff writer (not dated) on Indianmirror.com. Online at: http://www.indianmirror.com/ indian-industries/2012/fashion-2012.html

8. 'Fashion and lifestyle set to become a Rs. 394,000 crore market by 2020' by DNA correspondent, *DNA Daily News and Analysis* (March 16, 2016). Online at: http://www.dnaindia.com/money/ report-fashion-lifestyle-to-become-rs-394000-crore-market-by-2020-2189739

9. 'The State of Fashion' by Imran Ahmed, Achim Berg, Leonie Brantberg, and Saskia Hedrich (Business of Fashion and McKinsey

& Company, New York, December 2016). Online at: http://www.mckinsey.com/industries/retail/our-insights/the-state-of-fashion

10. 'Laboratories of style' and 'competent moderns' are both terms from Peter Bailey's seminal work on London's West End, *Popular Culture and Performance in the Victorian City*. Cambridge: Cambridge University Press, 1998.

11. From the Fashion United newsletter and fashion industry blog, see https://fashionweekweb.com/fashionweeks-around-the-world-list

12. 'The Ultimate Calendar of Every Fashion Week' by a staff writer at Vogue.com (February 1, 2016). Online at: http://www.vogue.com/article/fashion-week-dates-schedule-calendar

13. 'New high for corporate sponsorship at Lakmé Fashion Week (Curtain Raiser)' by IANS staff writer, *Business Standard* (August 23, 2016). Online at: http://www.business-standard.com/article/news-ians/new-high-for-corporate-sponsorships-at-lakme-fashion-week-curtain-raiser-116082300364_1.html

14. This means that many visitors come to see her when she returns to the village, so many that it is more economical to buy sweets in kilos rather than per piece.

15. For more on the idea of 'body work' see Carol Wolkowitz. 2002. 'The Social Relations of Body Work' in *Work, Employment and Society*, Vol 16 (3) Thousand Oaks: Sage Publications.

16. Cited in the essay 'Foucault, Femininity and the Modernization of Patriarchal Power' by Sandra Lee Bartky in I. Diamond and L. Quinby (eds). 1988. *Feminism and Foucault: Reflection of Resistance*. Boston: Northeastern University Press. For original source, see Simone de Beauvoir. 1952. (reprint 1988) *The Second Sex*. London: Picador.

17. 'Lean and mean: The looks that kill', by a staff writer, *Times of India* (April 13 2003). A student named Anjali Goyal was reported to have shot herself in April 2003 in New Delhi believing that she was too fat; she was 5 feet in height, weighing 50 kgs.

18. Ibid. This apparently has prompted public schools such as Delhi Public School to tie up with weight-loss clinics like VLCC (Vandana Luthra Curls and Curves Clinic) to draw up special diets for children which would be served in the school canteen.

19. 'Alma Gottlieb on Experiments in Anthropological Writing' by Rupa Pillai on AnthroPod: The SCA Podcast, Cultural Anthropology website (November 16, 2016). Online at: https://

culanth.org/fieldsights/990-alma-gottlieb-on-experiments-in-ethnographic-writing

20. In 2006 it was observed that organized retail was the fastest growing sector. KSA Technopak predicted that the annual market size would treble to over $21 billion by 2010. Just the top ten players, including Reliance Industries, Pantaloon, Bharti, Spencer's Retail and Tatas, would invest $18-20 billion in the next five years, and generate annual revenue of $50-60 billion. Pantaloon's retail space would go up from 4 million square feet to 30 million within four years. From 'Let's Talk Ten', cover story of Outlook magazine by Sugata Srinivasaraju (December 18, 2006) that focused on India's booming economy, then approaching 10% GDP. (For perspective, India's GDP in the first quarter of 2017 was 5.7%).

21. International designers state that most of the buying and orders from big retail chains and buyers come in before the fashion weeks are held nowadays. See 'The Catwalk, Darling? It's So Last Year' by Jess Cartner-Morley in *The Guardian* (October 13, 2003). Online at: https://www.theguardian.com/world/2003/oct/13/france.arts

22. "The Problem That Has No Name" was an essay in Betty Friedan's 1963 classic *The Feminine Mystique* (W.W. Norton, New York, 1963). It broke the myth of the happy suburban housewife in America and brought to light the hidden unhappiness of housewives, sold into the ideal feminine role of managing home and hearth.

23. Models' unions have been documented in some other parts of the world. In August 1993, traffic in Moscow was brought to a standstill by a demonstration of fashion models with placards that read 'Models get paid, not laid.' The gathering announced their intent to form a trade union to regularize pay and combat what they called 'sexual terror'. In the backlash that followed, the models were portrayed as hysterical, manipulative gold diggers. Undeterred, by spring 1994, they were working on a 'constitution'. The idea of a union was discarded, and instead they planned to establish a 'model's club' instead, which would allow a broader sphere of action and restrict membership to women only, unlike trade unions. Yet this too, failed.

     From Sue Bridger, Rebecca Hay and Kathryn Pinnkick. 1996. *No More Heroines? Russia, Women and the Market*. New York: Routledge.

24. From Dorian Leigh and Laura Hobe. 1988. *The Girl Who Had Everything: The Story of the 'Fire and Ice' Girl*. New York: Bantam Books

25. 'Eileen Ford: The Very Model of a Modern Model Agent' by a staff writer on Entrepreneur.com (October 10, 2008) Online at: http://www.entrepreneur.com/article/197628

26. 'The Rise and Fall of the Supermodel' by Seabastion on Belltory. com (March 3, 2010). Online at: https://bellatory.com/fashion-industry/The-Rise-and-Fall-of-the-Supermodel

27. 'Not a Pretty Picture at Elite' by a staff writer at *Bloomberg Businessweek* (June 14, 2004). Online at: https://www.bloomberg. com/news/articles/2004-06-13/not-a-pretty-picture-at-elite Also see 'Judge Orders Models Win in Agency Price-fixing Suit' by Anna Schneider-Mayerson in *Observer* (May 23, 2005). Online at http://observer.com/2005/05/judge-orders-models-win-in-agency-pricefixing-suit/

28. From her obituary 'Anjali Mendes, Pierre Cardin's Muse, Dies' by Anindita Ghose in *Mint* (June 18, 2010). Online at: http://www. livemint.com/Home-Page/PqCUZrJahO6myubieLt4LJ/Anjali-Mendes-Pierre-Cardin8217s-muse-dies.html

29. 'Anatomy Lesson', by a staff writer, *Indian Express* (The Sunday Express Eye, 18 September 2005). The author refers to this as 'the business of making perfect bodies out of rented parts'. Online at: http://archive.indianexpress.com/oldStory/78257/

30. A seminal essay on this is 'Emergence of the women's question in India and the role of women's studies' by Vina Mazumdar (Centre for Women's Development Studies, New Delhi, 1985). Online at http://www.cwds.ac.in/wp-content/uploads/2016/09/Emergence-Womens-Question.pdf

31. 'Feminist Thoughts from Here and There' by Nandita Gandhi, for Zubaan's Poster Women archive (August 4, 2011). Online at: http://www.posterwomen.org/Posterwomen/?p=5488

32. 'Changing the script: women and media in the eighties' by Pamela Philipose, for Jagori's Living Feminisms archive (not dated). Online at: http://www.livingfeminisms.org/story/changing-script-women-and-media-eighties

33. See Brinda Bose (ed). 2006. *Gender and Censorship*. New Delhi: Women Unlimited, for a range of debates on feminism and censorship in India.

34. 'India's dark history of sterilization' by Soutik Biswas for BBC News (November 14, 2014). Online at: http://www.bbc.com/news/world-asia-india-30040790

35. 'Glimpses of my journey' by Sarojini N. for Jagori's Living Feminisms archive (not dated). Online at: www.livingfeminisms. org/story/glimpses-my-journey

36. This was not without precedent. Similar protests had taken place the previous year. See 'A lobby of their own' by Arnab Neil Sengupta and Kai Friese for *India Today* (February 15, 1995). Online at: http:// indiatoday.intoday.in/story/moving-beyond-protest-marches-women-activists-spread-awareness-among-women-of-their-rights/1/288278.html

37. See Mary E. John's essay 'Globalization, Sexuality and the Visual Field' in Janaki Nair and Mary John (eds). 1998. *A Question of Silence: The Sexual Economies of Modern India*. New Delhi: Kali for Women, pg. 379. Online at: https://www.academia.edu/26044471/ Globalisation_Sexuality_and_the_Visual_Field_Issues_and_Non-issues_for_Cultural_Critique

38. 'How the Suffragettes used fashion to further their cause' by Cally Blackman in *The Guardian* (October 8, 2015). Online at: https:// www.theguardian.com/fashion/2015/oct/08/suffragette-style-movement-embraced-fashion-branding

    Also see some interesting images in 'Fashion and Women's Liberation' by Sara Bimbi in *Vogue* Italia (not dated). Online at: http://www.vogue.it/en/encyclo/fashion/e/fashion-and-women.

39. A significant number of women in sex work and in bar dancing were Dalit. Many of those who walked out were Dalit women leaders, who accused the others of being upper caste and class, and exploiting Dalit women's oppression. (Based on comments received from Laxmi Murthy and Jaya Sharma.)

40. Personal communication with sex workers' rights activist and leader at the conference, 12 September 2006, Kolkata.

41. An overlapping abbrevation of Bondage and Discipline (BD), Dominance and Submission (DS), Sadism and Masochism (SM).

42. 'Supermodel, refugee, UNHCR Ambassador: Alek Wek details the trauma of fleeing from war' by Chelsea Huang for Aol. com (September 22, 2015). Online at: https://www.aol.com/ article/2015/09/22/supermodel-refugee-u-n-ambassador-alek-wek-details-the-trau/21237618/

43. This clustering is not without a basis. Elements of their life such as stigma, the nature of dialogue with the family, their assumed 'hyper-sexuality', the social impact of their objectification, are reminiscent of similar tensions in other sexuality related

professions. For example, in *Gulab Bai: The Queen of Nautanki Theatre* by Deepti Priya Mehrotra (Penguin India, New Delhi, 2006) – a biography of Gulab Bai, a prominent nautanki (local travelling theatre/road-show dance form) artist from the northern state of Uttar Pradesh – the author recounts the lives of women nautanki dancers as being on a knife-edge between making independent sexual choices and the notion of sexual availability. In 'Dignity, No Bar' by Geeta Seshu for *The Hindu* (September 17, 2004) Varsha Kale representative of the Bar Girls Association fighting against the ban of dancing in dance bars in Maharashtra says, 'The bar girls have swollen feet as they stand in supposedly erotic postures and dance throughout the night. They ward off advances from customers and most of them are secretive about their work, even with their families, for fear of censure and rejection. The number of alcohol and drug abusers amongst them is high as they work in liquor and dance bars; and, worst of all, their work is dependent on the vagaries of youth and looks.'

Both the accounts sound suspiciously similar to that of many women in the fashion and modelling industry.

44. From the Editorial by Clare Hemmings and Amal Treacher to the issue on "Everyday Struggling" in *Feminist Review* number 82 (Palgrave Macmillan UK, Basingstoke UK, 2006); pg. 1-5.

45. *Vogue*, the international fashion magazine, with an India edition since 2007, has been making advertising films under the label #VogueEmpowers over the last year, keeping in tune with the general mood of the country that has been sensitive after a brutal case of gang rape of a student Jyoti Singh Pandey in 2012 in Delhi (called the 'Nirbhaya case' by media) that brought the city's young and women onto the streets to demand justice for sexual violence.

Acknowledgements

Gratitude twice over to those who were part of the PhD journey: first and foremost, the women at the centre of my research – my deepest thanks to all those who made the time to speak to me, and trusted me with their stories. Then: my PhD guide Professor MN Panini, and the faculty and staff at the Centre for the Study of Social Systems, School of Social Sciences in Jawaharlal Nehru University (JNU); the Indian Council for Social Science Research (ICSSR); the libraries at JNU, the Nehru Memorial Museum and Library, Teen Murti House and at the Jagori Resource Centre; the Fashion Design Council of India and Elite Modeling Agency India; the many friends who helped make Excel sheets, fix formatting glitches, forwarded me articles they felt would help, and proofread chapters at the last minute. That PhD really was a product of the kindness of strangers, the generosity of loved ones and the forbearance of friends.

This book however is a different beast, carried forward by a new set of friends and colleagues I found on moving to Mumbai in 2007. Thank you Nina Martyris, Sathya Saran, Sandhya Srinivasan, Hutokshi Doctor, Nonita Kalra and team at *ELLE* India, for giving a newbie freelance work as I tethered my ropes to this city. Because of you, I pushed myself to write for new audiences.

Thanks are due to The Hunger Project India, who commissioned a project that became my first book *Sarpanch Sahib*, and to the writers who agreed to be part of that book. They were important to my journey of becoming a 'writer'.

I'm so very grateful to the New India Foundation (NIF) and Ramachandra Guha, who gave this book a new lease of life when they awarded me with the NIF Fellowship in 2009. A dream fellowship that gave me a salary for a year to just sit and work on a book. I opened a small office with the stipend, and much of the ground work for this book was done during that year. Thanks to my office-mate, Rukmini Datta for co-creating a welcoming little space to write in.

The second lease of life came when Bishakha Datta introduced me to Jerry Pinto, whose sharp questions and firmness that I write and send him 1000 words a week jolted me from inertia. Jerry's insistence on a writing routine was a godsend and made me doggedly trot out the first drafts. Thank you Bishakha and Jerry.

Thanks are due to Geeta Seshu, who generously offered her office space for me to work on a round of the manuscript. And to Pradipta Sarkar and Amrita Mukerji, editors at the publishing house where this manuscript lay for a while, for their helpful comments on earlier drafts.

The Mont Blanc Writing Workshop I attended in 2016 became a turning point for me, and pushed me into a final, frenzied, delirious but delightful phase of working on this book. Thanks Michael Dahlie for the opportunity, Chris McMahon for the cheerful support, Cheryl Strayed for insights into her work, Pam L. Houston for being a fearless mentor, and all my writing group for their thoughtful comments on the chapter 'A Feminist at Fashion Week': James Joseph Brown, Brandon Dudley, Kari Shemwell, Caitlin L. Chandler, Lindsey Bennett Johnson, Ellie Rodgers, Betsy Marks Smith, Christopher Williams and Heidi Lender. And Gretchen Coombs, for her comments and companionship. Caitlin, Chris and Gretchen, thank you for your friendship, without which Chamonix wouldn't have been half as amazing.

I'm deeply grateful to feminist colleagues and friends who agreed to be interviewed and quoted for the last chapter, and spoke to me with such openness and honesty. Thank you Laxmi Murthy, Madhu Bhushan, Kalpana Viswanath, Nandita Gandhi, Nandita Shah, Mary John, Jaya Sharma, Rishita Nandagiri, Japleen Pasricha, Amena Azeez and Amba Salelkar. Thank you also to Vidyun Singh, Nonita Kalra, Sathya Saran, and Sushma Puri, who graciously reviewed their quotes after so many years and gave me permission to use them in the book.

In the last phase of the book, my thanks to Praneeta S Kapur and Devashri Mukherjee for reviewing the final draft, and to Anvita Madan Bahel, Gretchen Coombs and Bishakha Datta for feedback on the cover. Thanks to my work colleagues, especially Jacqueline Hart and Praneeta S Kapur for their support and understanding over the last two years.

Urvashi Butalia, my editor at Zubaan and the first to give me an authors' discount, made this book so much better, sharper and smarter. I felt that the manuscript had finally found a loving home in Zubaan. Thank you to Urvashi and the team at Zubaan for making the process smooth and enjoyable.

I'm grateful to my parents, Manjushree and Dipok Bhattacharjya, and my parents-in-law, Rekha and Arvind Gupta, for their solid support. They stood in gladly and unequivocally for me whenever required. Thanks to my parents-in-law for enabling me to travel for the writing workshop, and to my parents for their gentle encouragement as they diligently followed up on the book's progress every now and then.

I thank Tara and Arjun for their generous love and rejuvenating hugs. Tara's wise counsel on matters related to the book made me feel I had an ally in her, and Arjun made me smile often. I'm lucky to have them.

My gratitude to Saurabh Gupta, the perfect reading and writing companion, for joy every single day. Thanks for comments on early drafts, excellent conversations and being a true partner in every sense.

Thanks to you, the reader, for buying or borrowing this book. Please pass it on if you enjoy it. Find me on Facebook or Twitter or Instagram, because I know from past experience that some of you will.

Remember, there's a "j" in my surname.